KU-431-413

POPULAR GARDEN *PLANTS*

POPULAR

GARDEN PLANTS

An A-Z guide to your all-time favourites

DEALERFIELD

This edition specially printed in 1997 forDealerfield Ltd
Glaisdale Drive, Nottingham NG8 4GA, by
Marshall Cavendish Books, London
(a division of Marshall Cavendish Partworks Ltd)

ISBN 1–85927–014–X

Printed and bound in Malaysia

Some of this material has previously appeared in the Marshall Cavendish partwork *MY GARDEN*

CONTENTS

INTRODUCTION

Each profile is packed with information to help you select, buy and successfully grow a wide range of popular and easily available plants, from bright annuals to sturdy shrubs, and from tiny alpines and rockery plants to climbers and trees.

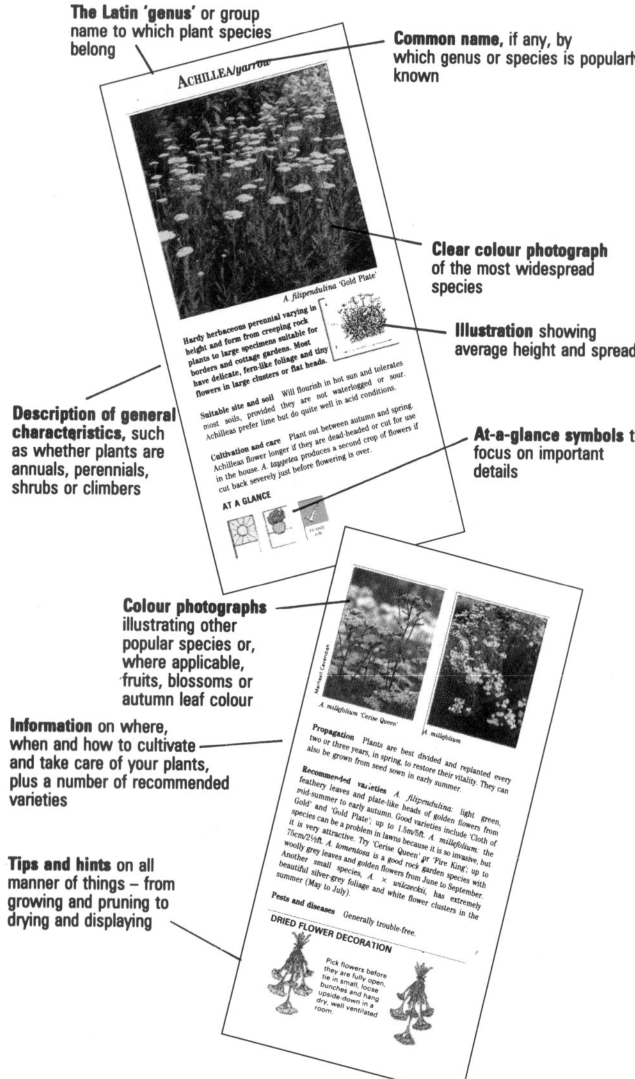

Use the information contained in the profiles to choose the right plants for your garden and, once chosen, to aid you in planting and aftercare. The book is a handy size – take it with you when you go shopping.

ALCHEMILLA/*lady's mantle*

A. mollis

Popular hardy perennials, grown for their attractive, curly-edged foliage as much as for their delicate sprays of tiny greenish-yellow flowers. Small, fine hairs give the leaves a silvery look and after rain they retain shimmering droplets.

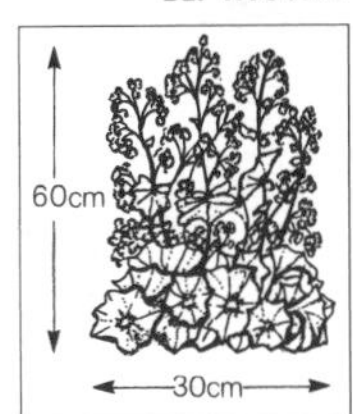

Suitable site and soil Plant in the front of herbaceous and shrub borders where they can spill out over a path, site them in a rock garden, or use as ground cover in partial shade. They need a well-drained soil; never plant in waterlogged ground. They tolerate a sunny position but prefer shade.

Cultivation and care Plant in spring or autumn and water in well. To prevent self seeding cut back flower stems to 2.5cm/

AT A GLANCE

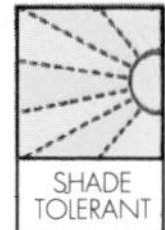

A. *erythyropoda*

A. *conjuncta*

1in above the ground in autumn before seeds ripen and fall or they can become invasive.

Propagation Alchemillas seed themselves freely if allowed to do so and can then be lifted and planted where needed. Alternatively, you can sow seed outdoors in the spring. Plants can be divided in spring or autumn.

Recommended varieties *A. mollis* has beautifully 'pleated' grey-green leaves and frothy sprays of lime green or sulphur yellow summer flowers. Height, 15-30cm/6-12in; spread, 45-60cm/18-24in. *A. alpina* has delicate, pale yellow summer flowers and is just 10cm/4in high; ideal for a bank. *A. conjuncta* is neat and clump-forming with greenish-yellow flowers. *A. erythropoda* has more unusual red flowers.

Pests and diseases Generally trouble free.

PLANTING TIP

Alchemillas have a sprawling habit, which makes them ideal for softening the edges of a straight path. Cut back if they start to become too straggly or unruly.

ALSTROEMERIA/*Peruvian lily*

Alstroemeria

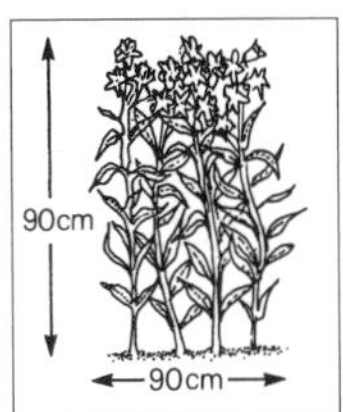

A charming group of herbaceous perennials that bear masses of small, lily-like flowers from June to August. Their bright petals are beautifully marked and carried on erect, wiry stems making them excellent for cutting.

Suitable site and soil Prefers a sunny, sheltered location on a well-drained, sandy, fertile soil. These plants look pretty in borders and are favourites for flower arrangements.

Cultivation and care Plant out young pot-grown specimens in spring. Handle the roots and shoots carefully as they are very easily damaged. Plant dormant tubers 15cm/6in below the soil surface in August or September and leave undisturbed for

AT A GLANCE

A.hookeri

A.pelegrina 'Alba'

several years. Fertilize in spring and water well during dry spells. Dead-heading is recommended.

Propagation Increase plants by careful division in early spring. Set in pots and grow on indoors before planting out in the autumn. Alternatively, sow seeds in peaty soil in a warm location in spring. Prick out and replant seedlings into pots and grow on for the summer.

Recommended varieties *A. ligtu* is the most useful species and hybrids and varieties of it come in shades of pink, yellow and orange, often spotted or streaked with a contrasting colour. *A. hookeri* has loose heads of orange and pink flowers, the upper petals blotched with red and yellow. *A. aurea* has orange flowers tipped with green and streaked dark red.

Pests and diseases Generally trouble-free.

WINTER PROTECTION
As these plants are not entirely hardy in cold areas, protect them during cold winter months by placing a mulch of straw, to a depth of 15cm/6in around the base.

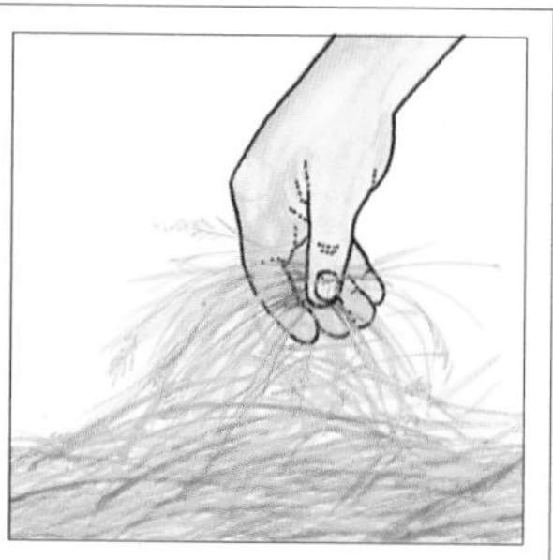

ALTHAEA/*hollyhock*

Althaea rosea

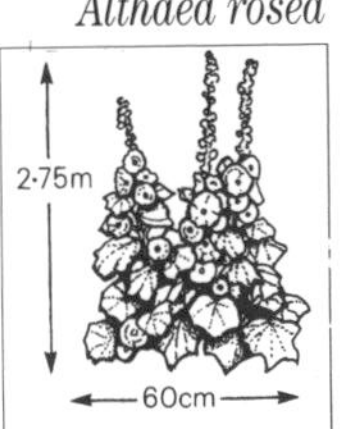

Tall, stately hollyhocks are classic cottage garden flowers. Available in a wide range of colours, these hardy perennials and biennials make a beautiful background plant for a display of summer bedding.

Suitable site and soil Choose a sheltered, sunny location with good air circulation and a rich, heavy, moist soil. Ideal for growing along a fence or wall to add tall interest.

Cultivation and care Plant out potted hollyhocks in spring, with the crowns slightly below the soil surface. Feed in early spring with a reputable brand of fertilizer and water well during dry spells.

AT A GLANCE

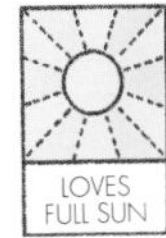

A. rosea

A. rosea 'Double Mixed'

Propagation Hollyhocks are best grown as biennials. Sow where you want them to grow in shallow drills 20cm/8in apart. Thin out to 60cm/2ft apart. Seeds can also be sown in a cold frame (if you have one) and transplanted in autumn to their final position, where they will flower the following summer.

Recommended varieties *A. rosea* has spikes of single flowers in a range of colours, including pink, yellow and cream. Look out for 'Chater's Double', which has rosette-like flowers and 'Majorette' and 'Summer Carnival', which have double flowers. They are available in mixed or separate colours, in shades of red, pink, purple, yellow, cream and white.

Pests and diseases Rust can be a serious problem (see below) but generally affects older plants. Diseased leaves should be picked off and burnt as soon as possible. Hollyhocks are also susceptible to attack by mildew.

CONTROLLING RUST ON HOLLYHOCKS

Rust shows as brown pustules on the stems and leaves of hollyhocks. Spores spread and can affect other healthy plants. Cut down and burn stems and leaves in autumn and pour fungicide on the crown.

ANEMONE/*windflower*

A. × ***hybrida***

A large group of graceful perennials, most of which bear shallow cup-shaped flowers. They bloom from early spring to late autumn and many have attractive seed heads and rich, dark green foliage. Anemones are fully- to frost-hardy.

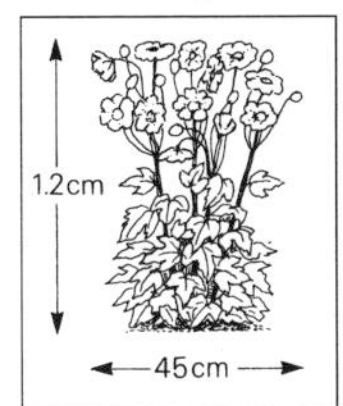

Suitable site and soil Anemones prefer a well-drained soil rich in humus. A limy soil will produce the best flowers on the tallest stems. Choose a naturalized, woodland setting or plant in mixed shrub and flower borders.

Cultivation and care Plant out spring-flowering tuberous varieties in late summer or early autumn. Summer-flowering varieties should be planted in spring or early summer.

AT A GLANCE

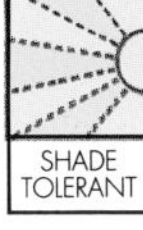

A. blanda 'Radar'

A. coronaria 'De Caen'

Propagation Divide clumps in spring, collect and sow seed in late autumn or take root cuttings from some types.

Recommended varieties *A.* × *hybrida* or Japanese species of anemones bloom in late summer and early autumn. Look out for reddish-pink 'Queen Charlotte', semi-double; white 'Honorine Jobert'. *A. blanda* blooms in spring, is perfect for a rock garden and is available in pink, blue and purple. *A. coronaria* 'St Brigid' comes in bright reds and blues, has parsley-like foliage and fresh tubers should be planted each year. *A. nemorosa* or wood anemone, is a woodland plant that naturalizes freely and is perfect in a partially-shaded location. *A. sylvestris* has carpeting, invasive fragrant white flowers in spring and early summer.

Pests and diseases Seedlings are prone to attack by flea beetles. Aphids may infest stems and leaves.

PLANTING ANEMONES

Plant all anemone tubers 5cm/2in deep and 10-15cm/4-6in apart in humus-rich, well-drained soil.

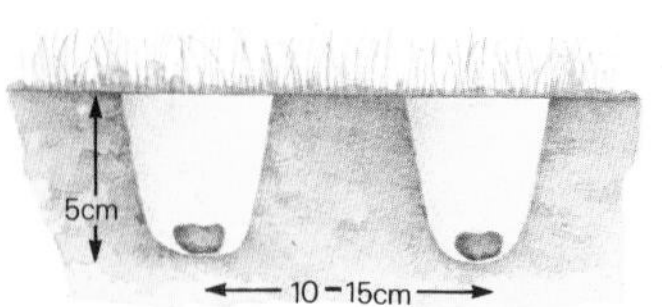

A. coronaria likes a sunny site while *A. blanda* and *A. nemorosa* prefer partial shade and look good in a natural 'woodland' setting.

ANTHEMIS/*camomile*

A. cupaniana

Carpeting and clump-forming hardy annuals, biennials and perennials grown for their daisy-like flowers and delicate, ferny foliage. Quick to spread, use to cover a bank or to fill gaps between paving.

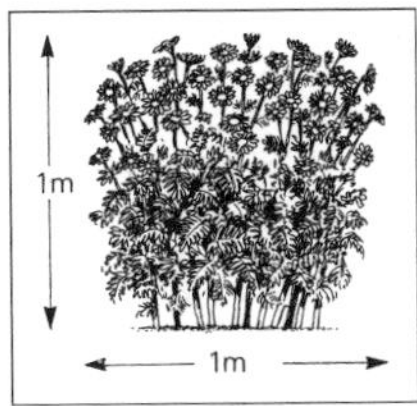

Suitable site and soil Select a sunny location. Soil should be well drained and not too fertile or plants may become straggly. Site low-growing varieties in a rock garden or in the crevices of an old stone wall or between paving.

Cultivation and care Plant out in spring, spacing 30-45cm/ 12-18in apart. Water sparingly and do not fertilize. Remove faded blooms to prolong flowering and reduce self-seeding.

AT A GLANCE

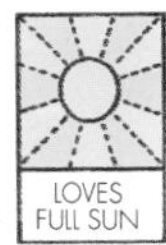

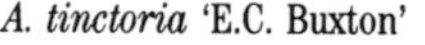

A. tinctoria 'E.C. Buxton'

A. nobilis 'Treneague'

Some varieties need to be divided every other year to prevent dead spots forming in the crown. In less sheltered areas, tall plants may need to be staked. Cut to ground level after flowering to produce profuse leaf rosettes during winter.

Propagation Divide clump-forming perennials in spring. Some species can be propagated by basal cuttings in late summer, autumn or spring.

Recommended varieties *A. tinctoria* is an evergreen, clump forming variety, with masses of yellow flowers in midsummer, and crinkled leaves. 'E.C. Buxton' has lemon-yellow flowers. *A. cupaniana* has dense, silvery foliage and makes an excellent cut flower; cut back after flowering. *A. nobilis* (common camomile) is mat-forming and has daisy-like flowers.

Pests and diseases Generally trouble-free

A CAMOMILE LAWN

A. nobilis 'Treneague' is a non-flowering ground cover plant that can be substituted for turf. It's ideal for soil that dries out too quickly for other grasses. Plant a whole lawn or just a small area.

ANTIRRHINUM/*snapdragon*

A. majus 'Harrisons Rust Resistant'

This delightful group of annual flowers covers a range of heights and flower types. They bloom from spring to autumn, bearing masses of flowers in a rainbow of colours, excellent for both formal and informal borders.

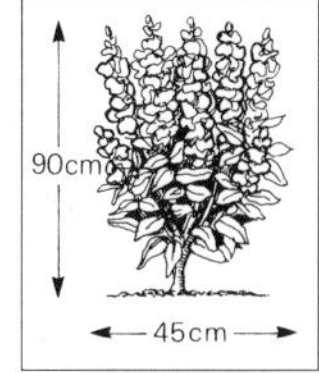

Suitable site and soil Select a sunny location on any rich, well-drained garden soil.

Cultivation and care Plant out in spring after danger of frost has passed. Dead-heading prolongs the flowering season.

Propagation Sow seeds outdoors in late spring or indoors in winter. Pinch out central tip when plants are 10cm/4in high.

AT A GLANCE

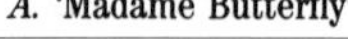

A. 'Madame Butterfly'

A. asarina

Recommended varieties *A. majus* is grouped according to size (tall, intermediate, dwarf) and flower type. 'Penstemon' indicates trumpet-shaped flowers, 'peloric' types have regular, tubular flowers and 'double' types have irregular-shaped flowers. 'Madame Butterfly' and 'Coronette' are both tall peloric types in mixed colours. 'His Excellency', has dense spikes of large, wide flowers and grows to a height of 45cm/18in. The 'Royal Carpet' series are dwarf, and are only 20cm/8in high while at the other end of the scale, the 'Supreme' series are very tall and impressive, with double ruffled flowers. *A. asarina* (also known as *Asarina procumbens*) is a trailing species that is especially suitable for planting in rock gardens, window boxes and hanging baskets.

Pests and diseases Rust disease may be a problem with *A. majus,* but there are plenty of rust-resistant cultivars available, so check when you buy.

SUCCESS WITH SEEDS

When growing seeds, use a compost made from equal parts of sand and moss peat. Place the compost in a seed tray or box and firm it down slightly, making sure it is level. Water the compost thoroughly using a fine rose and let it drain before sowing the seed. Cover the seed with a layer of fine sand, then place glass, clear plastic or cling film over the tray. Antirrhinum seeds are quick to germinate. As soon as the seedlings appear, add a liquid feed.

AQUILEGIA/*columbine*

A. vulgaris 'Long Spurred Hybrids'

These short-lived perennials look delicate but are very hardy. Sometimes known as 'granny's bonnet', they produce masses of airy blooms on slender stems from spring to early summer. The spurred flowers are excellent for cutting.

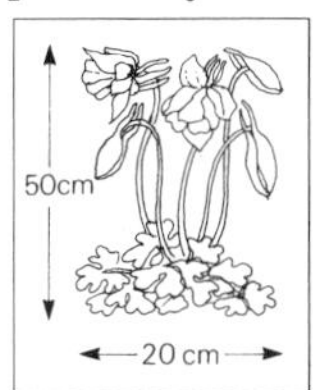

Suitable site and soil Use in beds and borders or in the rock garden. Ideal for naturalizing in semi-shaded 'woodland' gardens, but they are equally happy in sunny locations. Plant in well-drained soil.

Cultivation and care Plant out seedlings in autumn or spring. Water generously throughout the summer. Remove faded blooms to prolong flowering.

AT A GLANCE

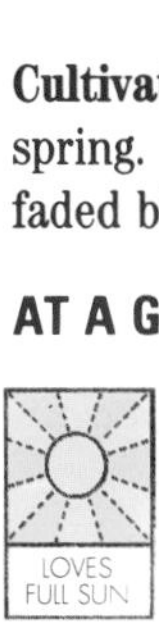

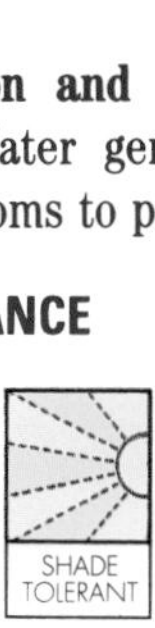

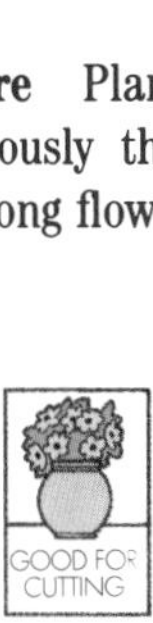

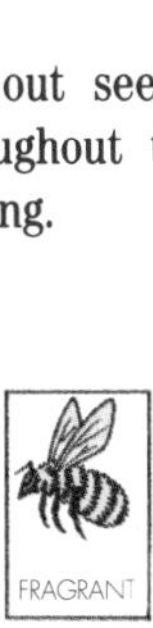

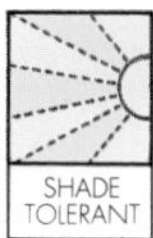

A. alpina

A. flabellata

Propagation Easy to grow from seed, indoors or out. Do not cover seeds with soil, as light is necessary for germination.

Recommended varieties *A. hybrida* has long, spurred flowers in a wide range of colours. 'Mrs Scott Elliot' and 'McKana Giant Hybrids' are particularly good. *A. vulgaris* is the old-fashioned columbine with beautiful dark blue, violet, pink or white flowers, it grows to 60cm/2ft. *A. alpina,* an ultra-hardy dwarf variety, is only 30cm/12in tall with lovely clear blue flowers. *A. longissima* has scented yellow blooms borne on tall, slender stems. The flowers appear from June to September and require regular dead-heading.

Pests and diseases Leaf miners may disfigure leaves. Spray with malathion in early, mid and late May (exact time may vary according to geographical location). Destroy infected leaves immediately – do not put them on a compost heap.

SURPRISES FROM SEEDS

Collecting aquilegia seeds from your garden may produce some nice surprises. Seeds from large, colourful hybrids will eventually revert, to produce old-fashioned columbines, which are smaller and more dainty. Try it and see!

ARTEMISIA/*wormwood*

A. arborescens 'Powis Castle'

This group of perennials, herbs and small shrubs are grown primarily for their rich, silvery foliage. Leaves are finely textured, often aromatic. Some varieties are evergreen. Few varieties have attractive flowers.

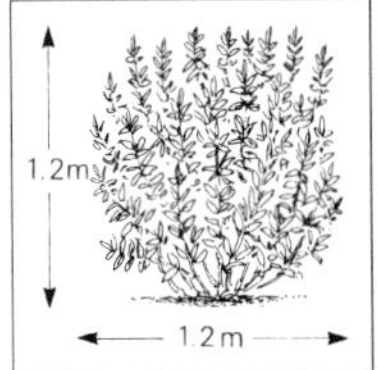

Suitable site and soil Plant in the front of borders, in an open location. Artemisias need full sun and perfect drainage. Poor, dry soils are best.

Cultivation and care Plant out in autumn or spring. Avoid over-watering or feeding. Protect plants in winter by surrounding with sharp grit or gravel. Trim lightly in spring and cut perennials down to ground level in autumn.

AT A GLANCE

A. arbrotanum

A. lactiflora

Propagation Divide and replant perennials between autumn and spring. Softwood or semi-ripe cuttings can be taken in summer from shrubby species. Take 5cm/2in cuttings and root in a light, sandy compost.

Recommended varieties *A. absinthium* 'Lambrook Silver' has silvery, aromatic, fern-like foliage. *A. abrotanum* (southernwood) has a bushy habit. *A. arborescens* is a small shrub with silvery white foliage and bright yellow flowers in summer; 'Powis Castle' is compact at 90cm/36in. *A. lactiflora* is a tall, green plant with decorative plumes of creamy white flowers in summer, ideal for fresh or dried flower arrangements. *A. stelleriana* is a tall, silver-leaved plant with yellow flowers.

Pests and diseases Watch out for cream-coloured root aphids on the leaves and spray with insecticide. The undersides of leaves may also suffer from rust.

SCENTED LEAVES

Plant artemesia beside a path, where it can be touched and its fragrance can be appreciated. With its silvery foliage, *A. absinthium* 'Lambrook Silver' is the perfect partner to purple sage and lavender.

ASTER/*Michaelmas daisy*

A. amellus 'Mauve Beauty'

These easy-to-grow herbaceous perennials have daisy-like flowers either singly or in sprays. Most flower in late summer or early autumn and are ideal for enlivening both the herbaceous border and the rock garden.

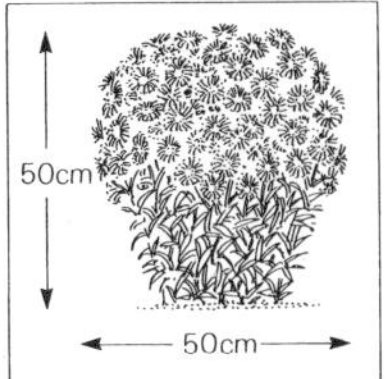

Suitable site and soil Asters are tolerant of most conditions except drought but prefer a sunny or partially-shaded site and fertile, moist but well-drained soil.

Cultivation and care Plant in groups of two or three. Stake taller varieties. Dead-head asters regularly or use as cut flowers. Never allow the soil to dry out completely. Cut down the stems of all plants in autumn.

AT A GLANCE

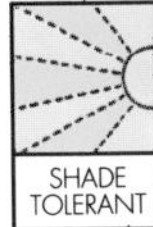

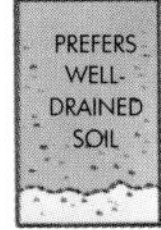

A. novi-belgii 'Carnival'

A. novi-belgii 'Marie Ballard'

Propagation Either by division in between autumn and spring or by softwood cuttings in spring. Large numbers of plants can be raised by teasing out roots into single shoots and planting them 15cm/6in apart in spring. Asters also self-seed.

Recommended varieties *A. amellus,* the Italian aster, is slow-growing to 60cm/2ft high. A. novi-belgii (height 1.2m/4ft) is the true Michaelmas daisy and includes 'Fellowship' with large pink flowers in autumn, 'Royal Velvet' with deep violet flowers, 'Royal Ruby' with deep red flowers and the dwarf 'Little Pink Beauty'. *A.* × *frikartii* 'Monch' (height 75cm/30in) has lavender-blue flowers with a yellow centre.

Pests and diseases There are generally no problems, but *A. novi-belgii* is prone to powdery mildew and insect attack. For the former, remove and burn affected leaves; for the latter, spray with soapy water.

THE PERFECT GIFT

With more than 500 species of aster, offering an enormous range of height, flower size and colour, there is bound to be one to please every taste. And as they are so easy to grow and propagate, there should never be any need to buy any once you have built up a stock. Increase your range by swapping with friends and sell spares at local charity fêtes. When you grow lots, you will also have plenty to cut and give away.

BEGONIA

B. × *tuberhybrida*

This diverse family of popular tender plants have bright and colourful flowers, and sometimes ornamental foliage. Though most are greenhouse or house plants, the types suggested here can all be used as bedding plants.

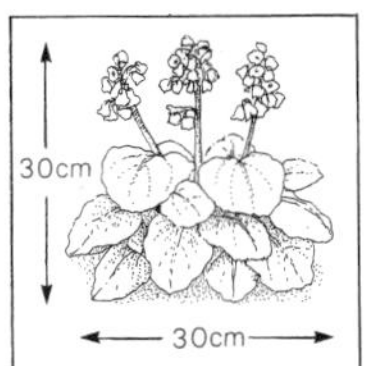

Suitable site and soil In containers, begonias grow well in any good potting compost. The fibrous-rooted *B. semperflorens,* and the bedding type of slightly taller tuberous-rooted begonias such as the 'Nonstop' range, do equally well in the ground in any normal garden soil. All prefer a sunny position, but they will also tolerate partial shade.

Cultivation and care The large-flowered kinds will produce

AT A GLANCE

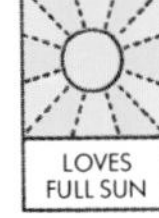

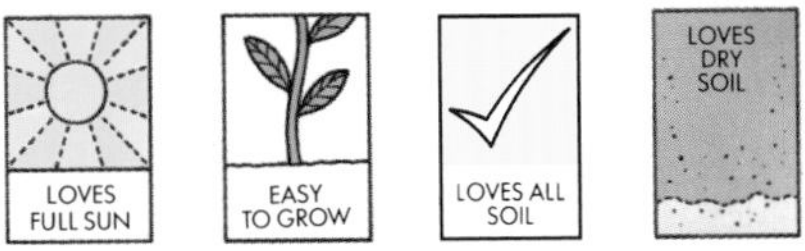

B. elattor hybrids

B. semperflorens

bigger and better blooms if the small flowers that appear behind the large central one are removed. Tuberous-rooted kinds are lifted before the first frost and the dried tubers stored in boxes of dry peat in a frost-free place. Fibrous-rooted kinds are best discarded.

Propagation *B. semperflorens* varieties are raised from seed sown in late spring. Some tuberous-rooted varieties, like the fibrous-rooted kinds, can be raised from seed. Other tuberous begonias are propagated from cuttings in spring.

Recommended varieties *B. semperflorens* has given rise to many varieties. For mixed colours, try 'Cocktail' or 'Supernova Mixed'. Tuberous-rooted bedding begonias have large flowers. Try any of the 'Nonstop' varieties for an extravagant show.

Pests and diseases Slugs are sometimes a problem.

POTS TO PLUNGE

Most bedding begonias are planted straight into the ground, but it is worth planting a few in pots to plunge into the ground or a window box. You can then take them indoors easily in the autumn where they will continue to flower for a little longer.

CALENDULA/*pot marigold*

C. officinalis

Pot marigolds are very easy to grow and will thrive almost anywhere in the garden. They make a profusion of seed and the yellow or orange daisy-like flowers open at dawn and close at dusk. They last well when cut.

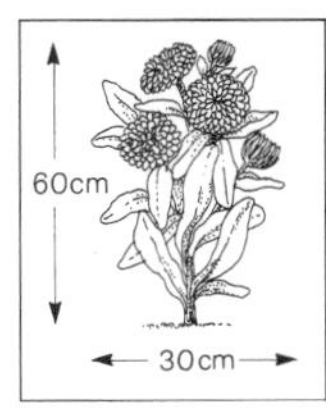

Suitable site and soil They will grow almost anywhere, including the poorest of soils.

Cultivation and care Space out to about 20cm/8in to allow the plants to grow freely. Keep the soil weed-free and dead-head the flowers to encourage a long flowering season and to prevent self-seeding – otherwise they will produce literally hundreds of self-sown plants.

AT A GLANCE

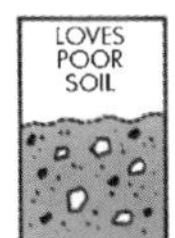

C. officinalis 'Pink Surprise'

C. officinalis 'Orange King'

Propagation Usually grown as hardy annuals, they can be sown outdoors in their flowering positions from spring. Alternatively, sow in autumn and place raised sheets of glass over them in winter for late spring flowering.

Recommended varieties *C. officinalis* has several strains, mostly sold as 'mixtures', to give a range of colours from yellow to bright orange. Most flowers are doubles, such as 'Pacific Beauty' or 'Art Shades'. 'Geisha Girl' is single, orange in colour, with in-curving petals. The dwarf 'Fiesta Gitana' form is neat and compact, useful for filling bare patches at the front of the herbaceous border.

Pests and diseases Cutworms and a variety of caterpillars can demolish leaves and stems. Powdery mildew is common, especially in late summer, and rust and smut fungi can cause spotting and discolouration of leaves in damp summers.

CHILDREN'S CORNER

Pot marigolds are really easy to grow. As they come up so quickly, they make ideal flowers for children to grow in their own little patch of garden, along with cornflowers and sunflowers.

Camellia

Camellia japonica

These deservedly popular, hardy evergreen trees and shrubs are grown for their glossy leaves and beautiful late winter and spring flowers, which come in a wide range of pinks, reds and white.

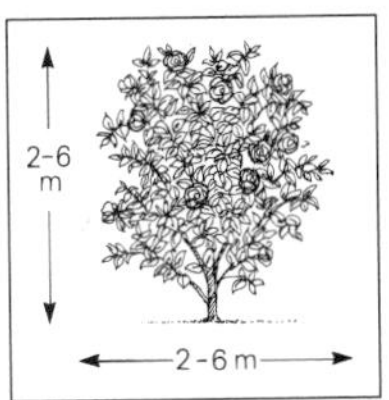

Suitable site and soil Camellias grow easily in lime-free soil enriched with leaf mould. Protect flowers from frost and early morning sun which may damage the blooms. Plant out of full sun as roots should be kept cool.

Cultivation and care Plant in spring or autumn. Dead-head after flowering and mulch well in spring using farmyard manure, leaf mould or lime-free compost.

AT A GLANCE

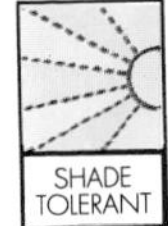

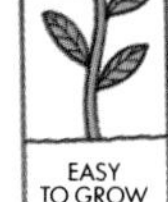

C. reticulata × *salvensis*

C. 'Nobilissima'

Propagation Root 7.5cm/3in cuttings in summer in equal parts of peat and sand. Keep at 16°C/61°F. Larger shrubs may be layered in the autumn. They will need about 18 months before being separated from the parent plant.

Recommended varieties *C. japonica* is tall, growing to a height of 2-6m/6-20ft. Red varieties include 'Adolphe Audusson' and 'Mars'; pinks include 'Gloire de Nantes' (rose-pink) and 'Magnoliaeflora' (pale blush pink); whites include 'White Swan' (pure white with golden stamens) and 'Nobilissima' (white peony-type flowers with yellow shading). *C.* × *williamsii* has glossy leaves and flowers from early winter to spring. One of the best varieties is 'Donation' with its big, delicately coloured, silver-pink flowers.

Pests and diseases Birds may damage the flowers. Frost will cause the buds to brown.

CAMELLIAS IN LIMY AREAS

Even if you have limy soil, this need not stop you growing a camellia. It makes a splendid specimen in a large pot or tub. Don't forget, though, it must have lime-free soil in order to grow happily.

CAMPANULA/*bellflower*

Campanula carpatica

These spring and summer-flowering annuals, biennials and perennials have delicate, usually blue, flowers. Use them in borders, rock gardens and as an edging to beds and paths. Many are suitable for cutting.

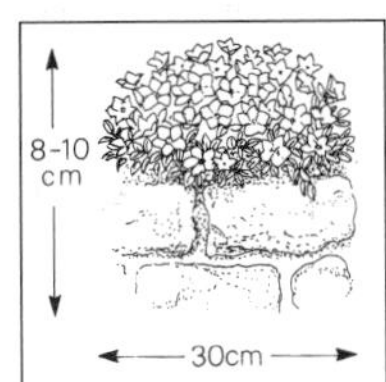

Suitable site and soil They prefer moist but well-drained soil and will grow in sun or shade, though you will find the colours look better in light shade.

Cultivation and care Plant between early autumn and spring. Taller varieties need support. Remove faded flower heads regularly.

AT A GLANCE

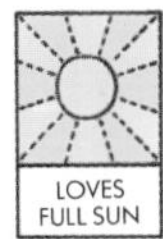

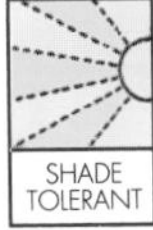

C. medium

C. latifolia

Propagation Sow seeds of perennials in pots in the autumn or spring. Plant out biennials and herbaceous plants in autumn. Plants with more than a single crown can be divided and replanted in either autumn or spring.

Recommended varieties *C. carpatica* (height 8-10cm/3-4in) is a perennial for edging or in a rock garden. It has large blue, white and purple flowers in midsummer. *C. latifolia* (giant bellflower) is a popular perennial with tubular flowers, (height 1.2-1.5m/4-5ft). 'Alba' is a white form. *C. medium* (Canterbury bell) has white, blue or pink bell-shaped flowers in late spring and early summer; height 30-90cm/1-3ft. *C. garganica* is a spreading perennial with small ivy-shaped leaves and clusters of pale lavender flowers in summer.

Pests and diseases Slugs and snails find the young shoots and leaves very attractive and palatable.

NATURALIZED CAMPANULAS

Like bluebells, campanulas look particularly attractive under trees and semi-shade brings out their delicate hues of blue. Plant them in a shady corner of the garden or let them peep out from under shrubs. *C. garganica* is particularly useful for naturalizing on a sloping bank or wall, while a grouping of different varieties can prolong the flowering season and add interesting contrast of height and colour within the group.

CHAENOMELES/*flowering quince/japonica*

C. japonica

The hardy, deciduous, slightly thorny shrubs produce masses of beautiful spring flowers, resembling apple blossom, in pretty shades of pink, red, white and orange. The yellow quince fruits appear in autumn.

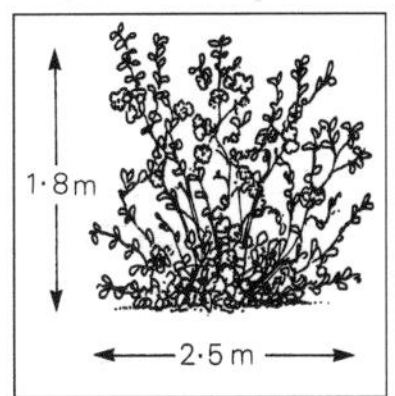

Suitable site and soil They grow in any except very chalky soil and prefer a position in full sun. They are happy in sunny borders or as wall plants.

Cultivation and care Plant in a sheltered sunny spot, from autumn to spring. After flowering, prune all shrubs. Train wall shrubs by tying the strongest shoots to the wall in a fan-like pattern in late summer and early spring.

AT A GLANCE

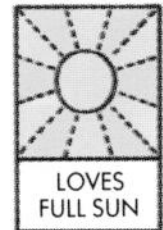

C. speciosa

C. × superba

Propagation Take heel cuttings in summer and insert in individual pots full of an equal mixture of peat and sand. Overwinter in a cold frame for planting out the following spring.

Recommended varieties *C. japonica* (height 1m/3ft, spread 2m/6ft) has brilliant orange and red flowers for two months from early spring. *C. speciosa* (height 2m/6ft, spread 2m/6ft) has fragrant fruits and is very free flowering. Its most popular forms include 'Moerloosii' with both pink and white flowers on the same branch and 'Nivalis' which has large pure white flowers. *C. × superba* (height and spread 2m/6ft) is a vigorous hybrid of the two. Varieties include 'Crimson and Gold' (crimson petals, gold anthers) and 'Hever Castle' (shrimp pink).

Pests and diseases On very chalky soils, chlorosis yellows the leaves. Fireblight can wither flowers and leaves.

QUINCE IN THE KITCHEN

The ripe fruits of *Chaenomeles* are very fragrant and make excellent jellies and jams. A spoonful of quince jelly in an apple pie is delicious. Wait until the fruit is yellow and fairly soft to the touch, otherwise it will taste very bitter. To make jelly cook the fruit first then strain it through a muslin bag to collect the juice. Jelly can be made from equal quantities of juice and sugar. Boil until a small spoonful of the mixture sets on a saucer. The jelly is also reputed to have healing properties.

CHAMAECYPARIS/*false cypress*

C. lawsoniana 'Ellwoodii'

These hardy evergreen conifers range from tiny specimens for troughs to medium-sized and large trees. Foliage colours include blue, gold and many shades of green. The foliage is soft and made up of flat fans of branchlets.

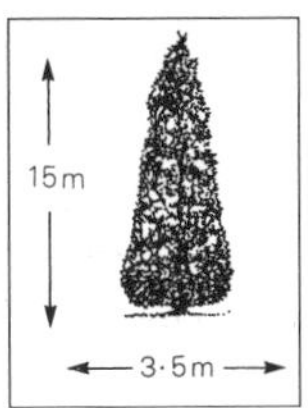

Suitable site and soil Their preference is for moist but well-drained soils. Drier sites or chalky soils produce tighter, slower specimens. Very dwarf kinds are best grown in gritty 'alpine' soils but must not be allowed to become too dry.

Cultivation and care As they will always be sold in pots, they can be planted out at any reasonable time of year. Water weekly (give a thorough soaking) in hot or dry weather.

AT A GLANCE

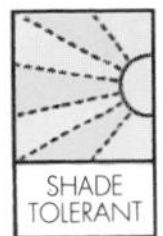

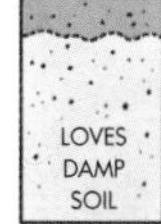

C. pisifera 'Boulevard'

C. obtusa 'Nana'

Propagation Difficult to propagate as special equipment is needed to take cuttings.

Recommended varieties *C. lawsoniana* 'Ellwoodii' is a medium-sized tree (2.4m/8ft after 10 years) that forms a bushy, grey-green column. 'Ellwood's Gold' is more compact with golden tips. 'Lane' has feathery, golden foliage. 'Minima Glauca' is a perfect, dark green globe suitable for a rockery. 'Pembury Blue' is medium, conical in shape and an outstanding silver-blue colour. *C. obtusa* 'Nana' is a very small, compact, dark green 'bun'; 'Nana Gracilis' is taller (90cm/3ft after 10 years), with similar foliage. *C. pisifera* 'Boulevard' is a medium size with steely, silver-blue, soft foliage that scorches in full sun. 'Filifera Aurea' is small to medium and conical and its branch ends are whip-like and gold.

Pests and diseases Trouble free.

TRUE OR FALSE?

It is worth making sure exactly what species your tree is before you attempt to move it. Chamaecyparis can be moved even when quite large, while the true cypresses (Cupressus species) are very temperamental and may die if they are moved or even clipped.

Cupressocyparis leylandii is a cross between the two and makes a fast hedge which is relatively tough. Take the tops out at the height you require and clip the hedge to create, then maintain, a good shape.

CHEIRANTHUS/*wallflower*

Cheiranthus

Deservedly popular, these late spring and early summer evergreens are perfect for beds, borders and containers. They are free flowering, have a heady scent and come in a wide range of beautiful colours.

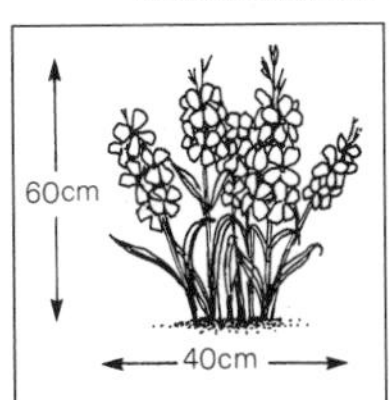

Suitable site and soil Plant in a sunny position in well-drained soil. Protect from cold winter winds or they may be damaged and flowering may be affected.

Cultivation and care Because they deteriorate with age wallflowers are usually treated as biennials, planted in autumn for spring flowering. Pinch out tips when plants are 15cm/6in to encourage a bushy shape.

AT A GLANCE

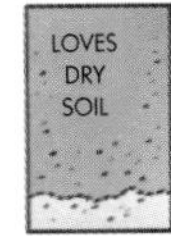

C. 'Fair Lady'

C. semperflorens

Propagation Sow seeds in late spring or early summer in an open seed bed, planting in flowering position in autumn. Take cuttings from varieties such as 'Harpur Crewe' after flowering.

Recommended varieties *C. cheiri* has very fragrant, colourful flowers with tall, medium and dwarf varieties. Tall varieties (height 60cm/24in) include 'Blood Red' (deep red), 'Cloth of Gold' (golden yellow) and 'Rose Queen' (rose pink). Intermediate types (45cm/18in) include the Fair Lady series (a mixture of colours), 'Primrose Monarch' (primrose yellow) and 'Ivory White' (cream). The dwarf Tom Thumb series (20cm/8in) come in a range of colours. *C.* × *allionii* (height 38cm/15in) is known as the Siberian wallflower and has slightly flatter flowerheads than the ordinary wallflower.

Pests and diseases A number of fungal disorders can affect wallflowers but they are generally trouble free.

FULL OF FRAGRANCE

Plant wallflowers where you will most appreciate their fragrance. They are happy in very poor soils so you can grow them in wide cracks in paving or walls, and next to the walls of the house – for instance, under a window or beside the front door.

Chrysanthemum

C. carinatum 'Court Jesters'

This very large and varied group of plants includes easy annuals and perennials for the garden as well as the well-known 'florists' chrysanthemums, some of which can be grown outdoors but are best left for the specialist.

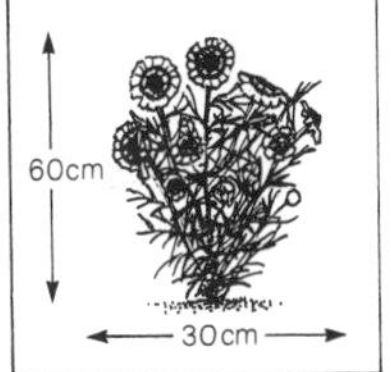

Suitable site and soil Annual and perennial kinds like a sunny site in a light, fertile, well-drained soil. The perennials are said to prefer lime, but this is not true in practice.

Cultivation and care Sow annuals in late spring where they are to grow. They will germinate in about 2 weeks and start to flower in midsummer. The taller ones (60cm/2ft) usually need the support of pea sticks. To obtain long flower stems for

AT A GLANCE

C. Gladys Sharpe

C. maximum 'Wirral Supreme'

cutting, pinch out the first flower buds. Cut back all perennial kinds to ground level in late autumn.

Propagation Take cuttings of perennial kinds 5-8cm/2-3in long from the base of the plant in mid-spring and insert in an equal mixture of peat and sand. Root on a cool window-sill. Established plants can be lifted and divided at the same time.

Recommended varieties Annuals: *C. carinatum* has flowers 5-8cm/2-3in across, with a purple central disc on stems 45-60cm/18-24in; seed strains include 'Merry Mixed' and 'Court Jesters Mixed'. Perennials: *C. maximum* (Shasta daisy) 'Wirral Supreme' is large and white (90cm/3ft); 'Snowcap' is very large and white (less than 60cm/2ft).

Pests and diseases Birds may damage the flowers. Frost will cause the buds to brown.

CREATING BIGGER BLOOMS

If you want really large flower heads on your exhibition type chrysanthemums you will need to cut off some of the side shoots. Simply break off the weaker shoots to leave five healthy ones on the plant.

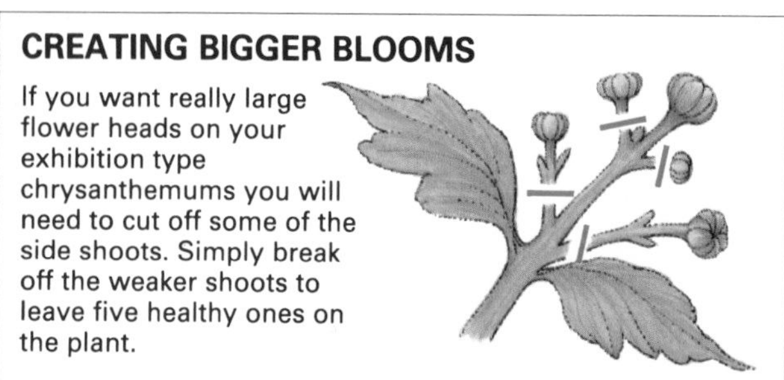

CISTUS/*rock rose*

C × *corbariensis*

These evergreen shrubs are suitable only for warm areas as they are not fully hardy. Their beautiful, short-lived flowers are borne in profusion in the spring and early summer and the flowers have a paper-like texture.

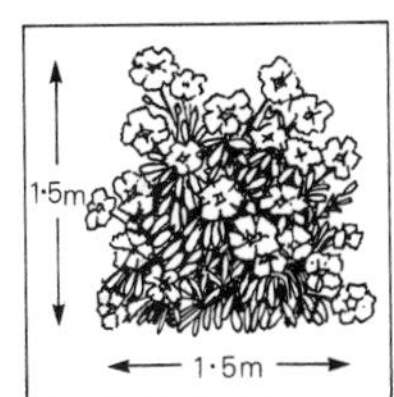

Suitable site and soil These plants need as much sun as possible and prefer a poor, dry soil with protection from the wind. They are ideal plants for hot, dry slopes, and will also grow happily by the sea.

Cultivation and care Plant in the spring, bearing in mind that once established, these plants do not like to be moved. Remove dead wood in spring but do not prune hard.

AT A GLANCE

C × *cyprius*

C. 'Silver Pink'

Propagation Growing from seed gives unpredictable results, so take heel cuttings in summer and protect through the winter in a cold frame, if you have one. Plant out in spring.

Recommended varieties *C.* × *corbariensis* is a spreading shrub with white flowers with yellow centres (height 90cm-1.2m/3-4ft, spread 1.8-2.7m/6-9ft). *C* × *cyprius* (height and spread 1.8m-2.4m/6-8ft) has large white flowers with a crimson spot at the base of each petal. *C.* 'Silver Pink' (height and spread 60-90cm/2-3ft) has clear pink flowers with golden stamens. *C. villosus* (height and spread 1.2m/4ft) has large rose-purple flowers. *C* × *skanbergii* (height and spread 90cm-1.2m/3-4ft) has clusters of pale pink flowers.

Pests and diseases They are generally trouble-free, though there is a danger of frost damage in cold areas, causing the shoots to die back. Protect in frost pockets.

PRUNING WINTER DAMAGE

Rock roses do not require much pruning as a rule. They are, though, liable to be damaged by cold winds so always position them in a sunny, protected spot out of danger from winds and frost. If your shrub does suffer from frost damage and some of its wood dies, this should be cut back in early spring before flowering. At the same time, cut out any straggly growth to improve the overall shape of the plant.

CLEMATIS

C. montana

These hardy climbers trail over pergolas, trellises, walls and trees. They climb using twining leaf stalks and need support at first. The large flowers range from white, through pinks, reds and blues to deep purple.

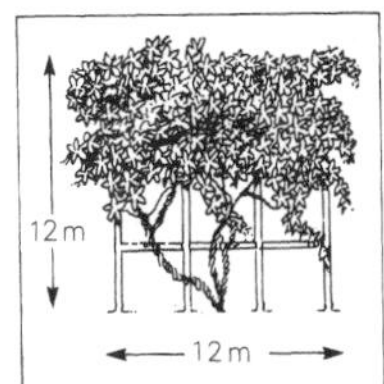

Suitable site and soil The roots need to be cool and moist but the plant should grow up into the sunlight. A few, such as 'Nelly Moser', need shade. Use manure or garden compost.

Cultivation and care Pruning is crucial. For species clematis, remove dead or weak wood and keep tidy. For large-flowered garden hybrids flowering in early summer, trim back old branches after flowering. For those flowering in late

AT A GLANCE

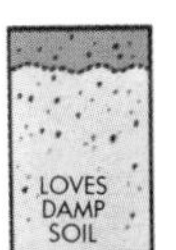

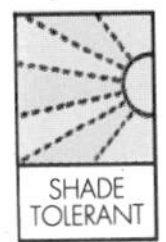

C. tangutica

C. Jackmanii 'Superba'

summer and autumn, prune hard to within 30cm/1ft of ground level in late winter or early spring.

Propagation Clematis is propagated by taking cuttings. Sowing seeds does not produce a true plant.

Recommended varieties The species clematis *C. alpina* is blue and flowers in spring. *C. montana* is white, though the variety 'Rubens' is pink and 'Elizabeth' has large, soft pink flowers. *C. tangutica* has smallish, 'lemon-peel' flowers in late summer. Among hybrids try 'Jackmanii Superba' with its large, purple flowers in midsummer, 'Henryi' which has large, white flowers in early to midsummer, or 'Lincoln Star' with pink flowers in early and late summer.

Pests and diseases Clematis wilt cause stems to rot and collapse. There is no cure, but avoid bruising stems.

PLANTING A CLEMATIS AGAINST A WALL

Dig a hole 45cm/1½ft square and 30cm/1ft deep and about 45cm/18in from the wall. Fill the bottom with well-rotted manure. Take plant from pot and place so that the top of the rootball is 2.5cm/1in below general soil level and the plant is leaning at an angle towards the wall. Place a cane at the same angle. Fill in and firm. Water with at least 9 litres/2 gallons and repeat regularly. Spray plant and surrounding soil with fungicide at the first sign of wilt, then cut plant back to a live bud or ground level.

CONVALLARIA/*lily-of-the-valley*

C. majalis

This hardy herbaceous perennial grows from a horizontal creeping root and has waxy, scented bell-shaped flowers on arching stems. It is small but can spread, making it ideal ground cover and for cutting.

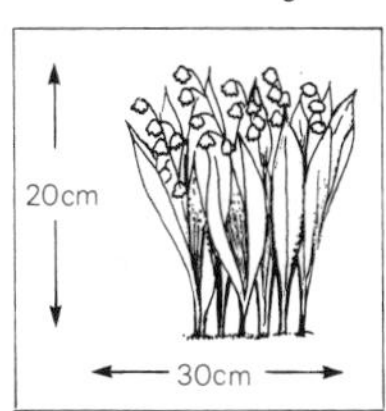

Suitable site and soil Lily-of-the-valley prefers light shade but can spread into full sun and thrive perfectly. It will grow in all soils but does not like bad drainage or the stickiest clays.

Cultivation and care Plant the crowns in autumn with the points just showing either singly 10cm/4in apart, or in small clumps of crowns about 20cm/8in apart. Avoid dry places and mulch every spring with leaf-mould or garden compost. It may

AT A GLANCE

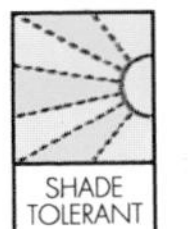

C. majalis 'Variegata'

C. majalis 'Rosea'

refuse to grow in the first place you try it, and even in the second. This is typical; persist until it takes. You can force convallaria for early flowering by lifting clumps in autumn and separating the crowns. Put them into pots and keep them in a cold frame or greenhouse until early spring, then bring them into a room with a fairly constant temperature of 20°C/68°F.

Propagation Divide between late autumn and early spring, lifting, splitting and replanting in dry, frost-free weather. Alternatively, seed can be sown thinly as soon as it is ripe.

Recommended varieties 'Fortin's Giant' has large flowers which are beautifully scented. 'Rosea' has lilac-pink flowers and does not spread nearly as widely as many other types. 'Variegata' has striped leaves.

Pests and diseases Plants in good soils are trouble free.

A PRETTY LITTLE POSY

When you are picking lilies-of-the-valley, pull the stems rather than cut them. They will last well in water. Pull up some of the leaves, too, to make a dainty arrangement, for a table centrepiece. Keep them away from glaring, artificial light.

Convolvulus

C. *tricolor* 'Royal Ensign'

This is a family of annuals, perennials and shrubs, both deciduous and evergreen. Some are hardy, others tender. The large saucer or funnel-shaped flowers last only for a day.

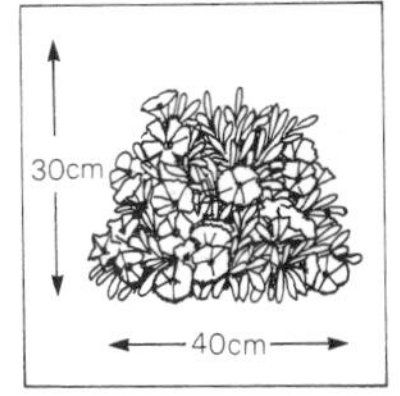

Suitable site and soil Grow in any ordinary or even poor, well-drained soil in a sunny position, well protected from cold winds. Rock gardens and banks are suitable for smaller varieties. Grow climbing forms over walls, fences, arches, a trellis or a hedge alone or with other climbers.

Cultivation and care Dead-head frequently for continuous flowering from early summer through to the autumn.

AT A GLANCE

C. *cneorum*

C. *althaeoides*

Propagation The seeds of annuals should be sown under glass in seed compost. Early spring is the best time to do this, and John Innes compost is sufficient. You can also wait until mid-spring to sow the seeds in the site chosen for flowering. Take heel cuttings of shrubby and perennial species in summer. Overwinter in a cold frame, if you have one, and plant out the following spring.

Recommended varieties *C. tricolor* (also known as *C. minor*) is a fast-growing hardy annual (height 30cm/12in; spread 30-40cm/12-16in) with blue flowers with yellowish throats. *C. cneorum* is a half-hardy evergreen shrub with pink buds opening to white flowers. (Height and spread 60-90cm/2-3ft.) *C. althaeoides* is a prostrate perennial with silvery green leaves and pale pink flowers.

Pests and diseases Generally trouble free.

A SUNNY BANK

Like its fast growing cousin, morning glory (ipomoea), *C. althaeoides* will creep if it is not supported. If you have a dry sunny bank with poor soil, *C. althaeoides* will quickly clothe it in pale pink flowers from summer to autumn transforming an otherwise barren part of the garden. In order to make sure the bank is covered all year round grow it with an evergreen such as purple aubrieta which begins flowering in spring and will blend with the pink convolvulus in summer.

COTONEASTER

C. horizontalis

A range of shrubs ranging from prostrate mat-forming types to small trees with brilliant autumn colour in their leaves or fruit and white or pink flowers in the spring and early summer.

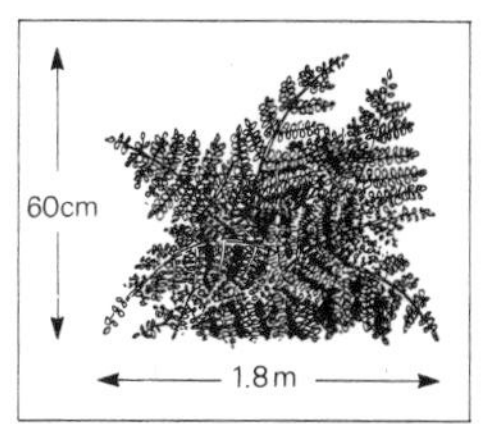

Suitable site and soil Deciduous species grow well in full sun but evergreens will tolerate shade. They all prefer well-drained soil. Some forms are suitable for hedging or ground cover.

Cultivation and care Most forms can be rejuvenated and neatened by being trimmed. Prune young plants for hedges to encourage bushing out.

AT A GLANCE

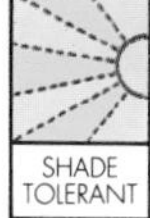

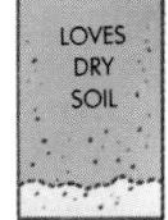

C. conspicuus

C. microphyllus

Propagation You can grow new plants from the berries but this can mean a long wait for results. Semi-ripe cuttings or layering are preferable.

Recommended species *C. horizontalis* (herringbone cotoneaster) is a low-growing deciduous shrub (height 60cm/2ft, spread 1.8m/6ft) with herringbone branches, pink spring flowers followed by red berries and rich autumn foliage. *C. conspicuus* is an evergreen shrub (height 1.8m/6ft) with arching branches and a profusion of both white flowers and red fruits. *C. microphyllus* is a dwarf, glossy-leafed evergreen with white flowers, large bright red berries and is good for ground cover.

Pests and diseases Fireblight can blacken and wither flowers and foliage. Honey fungus kills plants quickly. Birds are greatly attracted to the berries.

AN INVALUABLE WALL SHRUB

C. horizontalis will spread its way across a wall or bank, covering it with rich autumn colour, as well as scarlet berries and spring flowers. It will also do well on quite a cold wall in shade.

CROCOSMIA/*montbretia*

C. 'Lucifer'

Strictly speaking 'bulbs' (actually corms), but treated as fleshy-rooted, hardy perennials. They have iris-like foliage, and trumpet-shaped scarlet, orange-red and yellow flowers in late summer/early autumn.

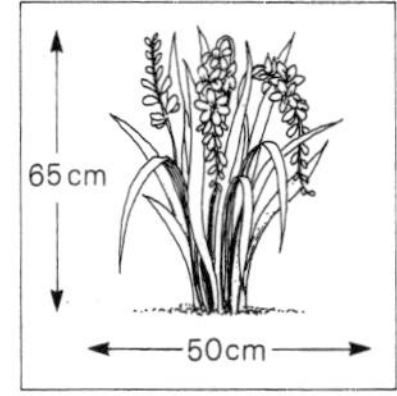

Suitable site and soil All well-drained garden soils except really stiff clay are suitable. In mild areas the old-fashioned common montbretia can be invasive in sun or part shade but modern hybrids prefer full sun and are good border plants.

Cultivation and care Crocosmias can be left alone without attention for many years and will continue to flower happily.

AT A GLANCE

C. 'Emily McKenzie'

C. 'Solfataire'

Propagation Easy by simple division in early spring. Replant the divisions immediately.

Recommended varieties The common montbretia is *Crocosmia* × *crocosmiiflora*, with nodding, vermilion-orange flowers, but it usually confused with the similar *C. masonorum*, whose flowers look up. Most of the varieties sold are hybrids, such as 'Bressingham Beacon' with orange buds opening to bicoloured yellow and orange flowers, growing to 90cm/3ft in summer; 'Citronella' with yellow flowers, growing 60cm/2ft in mid to late summer; 'Emily McKenzie' with nodding dark orange flowers, but non-invasive, growing to 60cm/2ft in mid to late summer; 'Lucifer' with brilliant scarlet flowers, growing to 120cm/4ft early summer; 'Solfataire' with apricot-yellow flowers, growing to 60cm/2ft in mid to late summer.

Pests and diseases Trouble-free.

COLOUR MIXES

Cool and integrate the bright oranges and reds of montbretia by planting them with blue flowers (agapanthus, summer caenothus), soft yellow flowers (for example, varieties of hemerocallis) and/or silver foliage.

Crocus

C. vernus 'Queen of the Blues'

These well-known, early spring flowers grow from corms. There are several different groups, including the Dutch crocus, the smaller Chrysanthus types, and the true autumn-flowering crocuses.

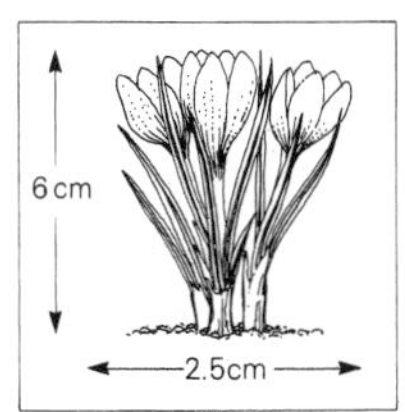

Suitable site and soil Always choose a sunny position where the corms can be warm and dry in summer. The composition of the soil does not matter as long as it is very well drained and is not heavy clay. On wet, sticky soils, grow in raised beds.

Cultivation and care Plant with about 2.5cm/1in of soil above the top of the corm and leave them gradually to make clumps. Make sure that the leaves do not become damaged or

AT A GLANCE

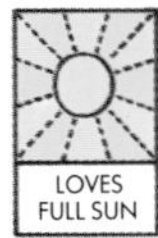

C. chrysanthus 'Snowbunting'

C. chrysanthus 'Bluebird'

removed until seven weeks after the last flowers have faded, as they are needed to feed the corms.

Propagation Buy inexpensive corms. Plants raised from seed will flower after three years.

Recommended varieties Large-flowered (Dutch) crocus flowers in early spring; 'Queen of the Blues' has very large soft blue flowers; 'Snowstorm' has large, globular, pure white flowers; 'Remembrance' is soft purple. *C. chrysanthus* crocuses flower a little earlier than the Dutch type. The many varieties include 'Advance' (yellow and bronze), 'Snowbunting' (white) and 'Bluebird' (white inside, blue outside). *C. speciosus* varieties flower in the autumn.

Pests and diseases Sparrows often attack yellow crocus flowers. Mice sometimes eat the corms.

TRUE OR FALSE?

The true autumn crocus, *Crocus speciosus* (right), is not related to *Colchicum autumnale*, though this is also commonly known as autumn crocus. Both look similar and both grow from corms.

Cyclamen

C. hederifolium

Hardy cyclamen are plants for the open garden and quite different from those grown as house plants. They are smaller, neater, and do not need the attention given to indoor species of cyclamen.

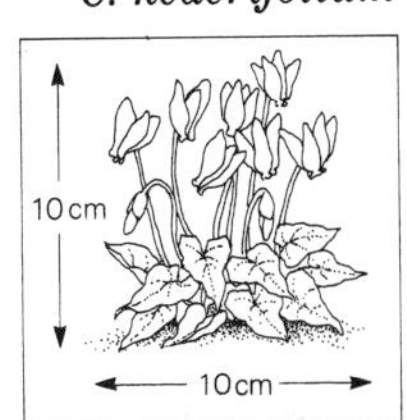

Suitable site and soil The ideal soil contains plenty of leafy material and is friable (not necessarily light, but certainly not sticky). Cyclamen vary in their requirements, but in general they are ideally sited in semi-shaded places.

Cultivation and care Ideally, you should buy cyclamen growing in a pot. Transplant so that the soil level is the same. Dried corms are inexpensive alternatives but take time to establish:

AT A GLANCE

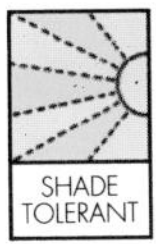

C. coum

C. repandum

plant them on their sides with no more than an inch of soil above them, except for *C. repandum,* which should be about 7.5cm/3in deep.

Propagation Collect seed as soon as the capsules burst and sow it immediately in pots. Prick out after two years.

Recommended varieties *C. neapolitanum* (syn. *C. hederifolium*) is autumn flowering with pink or white flowers, patterned leaves, and is very hardy. The winter-flowering *C.coum* has several forms with red, pink or white flowers and is very hardy. The spring-flowering *C. repandum* has fragrant pink, carmine or white flowers but needs a mild area. The late summer/early autumn flowering *C. europeum* (syn. *C. purpurascens*) has scented pink to carmine flowers and is hardy.

Pests and diseases Hardy cyclamen are trouble-free.

A LOVELY SITE

Cyclamens are at their loveliest when planted around the root base of shady trees but they must be given a leafy or peaty soil initially and watered well until established, if they are to develop and grow satisfactorily.

CYTISUS/*broom*

C. scoparius 'Dragonfly'

Cytisus **plants are commonly known as 'brooms'.** ***Cytisus*** **species and varieties vary from tiny shrubs for the rock garden to small trees. They have pea-shaped flowers that are usually, but not always, yellow.**

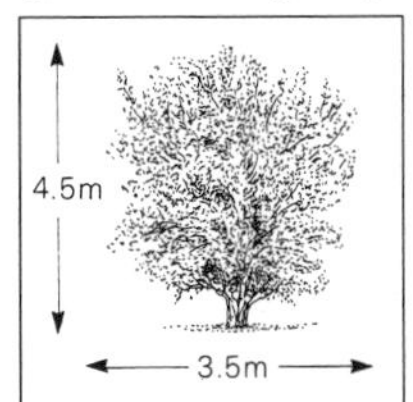

Suitable site and soil Broom species are hardy and will grow on all garden soils. Most of the hybrids, however, including those of the common broom, fail on shallow soils over chalk. They are all excellent for clay and like full sun.

Cultivation and care Brooms are effective though short-lived shrubs and are excellent for planting in new gardens. Life is extended if they are pruned back after flowering.

AT A GLANCE

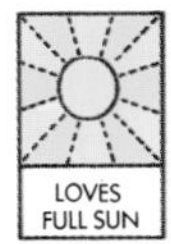

C. battandieri

C. × *kewensis*

Propagation Soak seeds in warm water and leave for 24 hours. Sow in late winter and germinate at 18°C/65°F or in early spring and place in a cold frame. Half-ripe, heeled cuttings, taken in late summer, root slowly in a frame.

Recommended varieties *C. ardoinii:* dwarf (heights 5-10cm/2-4in), alpine shrub with yellow flowers in spring. *C. battandieri* (pineapple broom): wall shrub, with large, three-lobed, intensely silver leaves and large clusters of yellow, pineapple-scented flowers in summer (height 4.5m/15ft). '*C.* 'Burkwoodii': hybrid with cerise and crimson flowers in late spring. *C.* × *kewensis*: wide, low shrub (height 60cm/2ft) with creamy-white flowers in spring. *C. scoparius* (height 2.4m/8ft) is the common broom and good varieties include 'Cornish Cream' and 'Dragonfly.'

Pests and diseases Trouble-free.

PRUNING BROOM

Broom that flowers on last year's wood should be cut back by two-thirds after flowering. Prune species that flower on the same year's growth just before the growing season starts in early spring.

Dahlia

D. 'Bishop of Llandaff'

These come in a range of flower shapes, styles and colours and are one of the most popular late summer plants. Border dahlias are named varieties propagated by cuttings while bedding dahlias are smaller and usually grown from seed.

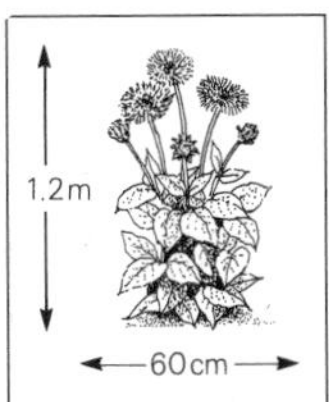

Suitable site and soil Dahlias need a sunny position and well-drained soil. Give border dahlias 110gm/4oz per sq.m. of bonemeal when planting. For bedding and border dahlias dig in well-rotted manure the previous autumn.

Cultivation and care Plant tubers of border dahlias in spring 10cm/4in deep. Put stakes in position before planting. Pinch out leading shoots one month after planting. In autumn,

AT A GLANCE

D. 'Coltness Hybrid'

D. 'Redskin'

let tops become frost blackened, then cut down stems and lift tubers for frost-free storage.

Propagation Place tubers in 50/50 moist peat and sand in early spring with crowns above the surface. When the buds begin to swell, divide the tubers with a sharp knife. Sow bedding dahlias in late winter in boxes, germinate at 15°C/60°F, prick out into individual pots, plant in late spring.

Recommended varieties There are too many border dahlias to list but the good for planting with other herbaceous plants are the peony-flowered kinds such as 'Bishop of Llandaff' and 'Orange Flora'. Bedding dahlias: seed strains 'Early Bird Mixed' and 'Redskin' are easy to grow and germinate.

Pests and diseases Grey mould and sclerotinia rot can affect border kinds. Aphids and earwigs can be a problem.

OVERWINTERING TUBERS

After frost has discoloured the foliage, lift the tubers carefully and leave upside down for a week while water stored in the stems drains out. Keep the tubers in a box just covered with peat where they will not be damaged by frost.

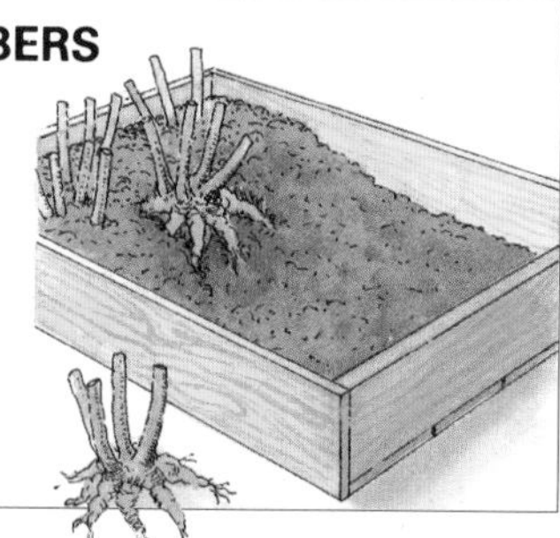

Daphne

D. × *burkwoodii* 'Somerset'

These dwarf to medium-sized, hardy shrubs, evergreen or deciduous, have large clusters of flared, tubular, highly-scented flowers. The flowers are usually pink or reddish-purple, but can be white or yellow-green.

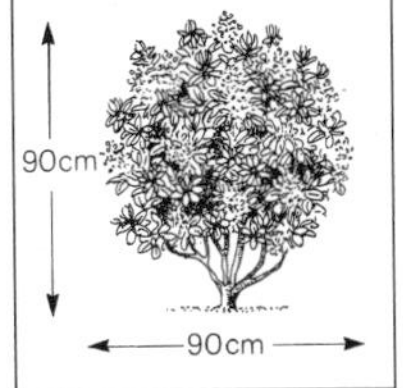

Suitable site and soil All good, well-drained soils are suitable, with some moisture, but not wetness. All except *D. blagayana* which requires shade, should have some sun or light shade.

Cultivation and care Plant in spring. Cover the root area of all except *D. blagayana* and *D. cneorum* with flat stones for a cool root run. Root their branches by burying them in peaty,

AT A GLANCE

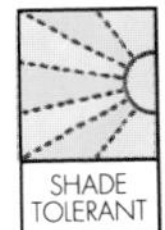

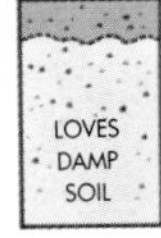

D. blagayana

D. mezereum

sandy compost so that just the terminal clusters of leaves show or they can become straggly and short lived.

Propagation Take semi-ripe cuttings of side shoots in late summer in 50/50 sand and peat mixture in a cold frame. Pot up the following spring and plant out after two years. Sow seeds as soon as ripe, leave in a cold frame and keep moist.

Recommended varieties *D. blagayana* is a mat-forming, deciduous shrub with creamy-white flowers in spring (height 30cm/12in). *D. × burkwoodii* (height 90cm/3ft) is semi-evergreen with pink flowers in late spring. *D. cneorum* is a mat-forming, evergreen with rose-pink flowers in late spring (height 15cm/6in). *D. mezereum* (height 90cm/3ft) is a deciduous shrub with rose-pink flowers in early spring.

Pests and diseases Rare, viral stunting and distorting.

PROLONGING SHRUB LIFE

Cover the branches of *D. cneorum* with compost to layer them. This is an example of mound layers but in the case of daphnes, it is used to promote the long life, and appearance, of the plant rather than for propagation purposes.

Delphinium

D. 'Blue Heaven'

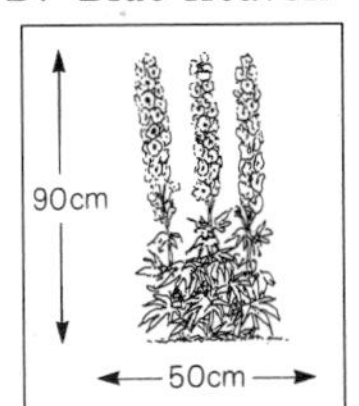

The tall hybrid delphiniums are hardy, herbaceous, summer-flowering perennials and favourites for a cottage-garden look. Flower colours are mostly blue, white, and blue-mauve. The flower spikes are carried on long stems.

Suitable site and soil Give delphiniums a sunny border with deep, rich soil and shelter from wind. They do not like extremely acid soils and prefer neutral to limy ones.

Cultivation and care Plant out from autumn to early spring in groups of three or more. Set strong stakes in mid-spring. After flowering, cut back to a strong leaf to produce a second blooming. Cut to ground level in autumn.

AT A GLANCE

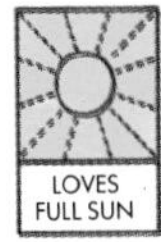

D. 'Pacific Rose'

D. 'Butterball'

Propagation Take 10cm/4in cuttings of new spring growth as close to the roots as possible and insert in 50/50 mixture of peat and sand in a cold frame. Transplant in late spring to a nursery bed and plant in permanent positions in autumn. Sow seed as soon as possible, as it does not keep.

Recommended varieties *D. elatum* has 1-1.5m/3-5ft flower spikes and most garden varieties derive from it including 'Belladonna Improved', blue, white and pink (height 90cm/3ft); 'Dwarf Blue Heaven', sky-blue, single flowers, no staking; 'Pacific Giant Mixed' and other 'Pacific' strains, blue, mauve, chocolate, white, semi-double and single flowers; 'Butterball', cream; 'Moonbeam', white, 'Loch Leven', sky-blue.

Pests and diseases Slugs and snails may be a problem. Various rots and powdery mildew occur on plants in poor soils or extremes of wetness or dryness.

CREATING A COTTAGE GARDEN BORDER

Delphiniums are perfect flowers for the cottage garden look. As they are so tall, plant them at the back and fill the foreground with sweet peas, pinks, peonies and other old-fashioned favourites.

DIANTHUS/*pink/carnation/sweet William*

D. barbatus

Dianthus is a very large family of colourful, often scented perennials for almost any sunny spot in the garden. The flowers are single or double and range from red to delicate pinks and white.

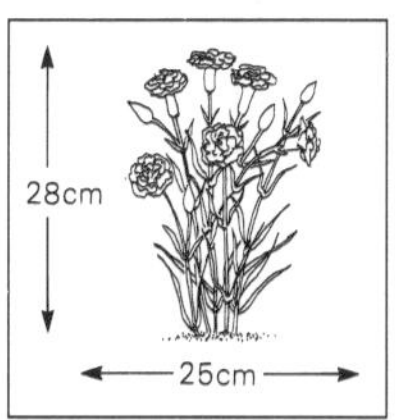

Suitable site and soil Sun and well-drained soil. The smallest species and hybrids are excellent for rock gardens, troughs and raised beds. Pinks and annual and border carnations like border conditions enriched with rotted manure.

Cultivation and care Plant rock garden pinks in spring, border pinks and carnations in autumn or spring. Add lime if soil is acid. Stake taller varieties for the first year. In spring,

AT A GLANCE

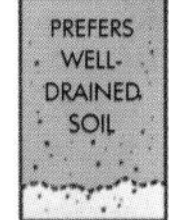

D. × *allwoodii* 'Doris'

D. caryophyllus 'Robin Thain'

pinch off the main shoot tip of young border pinks just above a leaf joint; remove all except main or side shoot buds of carnations. Plant sweet William seedlings in autumn.

Propagation For rock garden hybrids and all garden pinks, take cuttings in midsummer 8cm/3in long. Layer border carnations in midsummer. Separate at the end of summer, lift and plant in autumn. Sow annual carnations in gentle heat in early spring. Sow sweet William outdoors in early summer.

Recommended varieties The choice is endless and all good seed catalogues have first-class strains. Consider colour and scent as well as size: sweet Williams (*D. barbatus*) grow to about 30-60cm/1-2ft; border pinks 25-35cm/10-14in; border carnations 90cm/3ft; and annual carnations 30cm/12in.

Pests and diseases Aphids can be a problem.

STOPPING PINKS

Garden pinks should be stopped in early spring. This means you snap off the tops of main stems just above a leaf joint to encourage side shoots to produce more plentiful flowers.

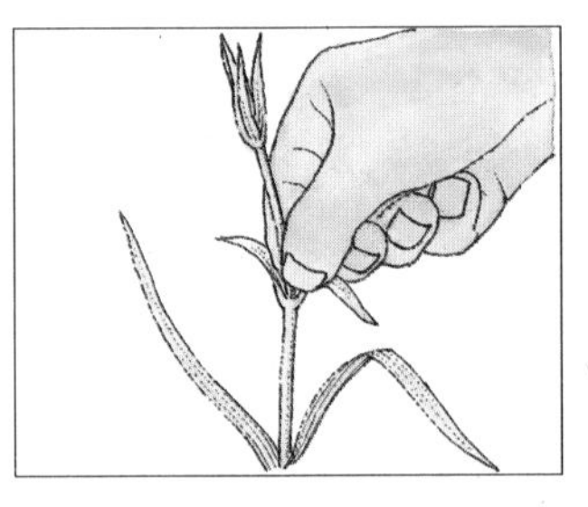

ERICA/*heather/heath*

E. carnea 'Myretoun Ruby'

The mostly hardy evergreen shrubs and sub-shrubs of the Erica genus, known as heathers, are grown for their bell-shaped flowers and attractive foliage and are used as ground cover and hedging.

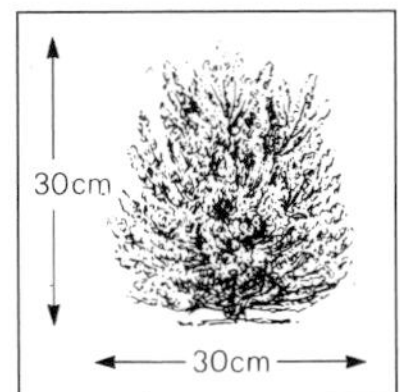

Suitable site and soil Although tolerant of many soil types, they do best in peaty acid soils in an open, sunny spot.

Cultivation and care Be sure to clear up any fallen leaves from around Ericas. Plant out in spring or autumn, or container plants at anytime. Trim tall-growing varieties lightly in autumn or before new growth starts. Clip off the dead flower stems of summer-flowering Ericas close to the foliage in

AT A GLANCE

E. carnea 'Springwood White'

E. cinerea 'Purple Beauty'

spring. Cut back winter and spring-flowering plants after flowering. Water in spring and during dry periods.

Propagation By cuttings in summer and early autumn. Large plants can be propagated by layering from early spring.

Recommended varieties *E. carnea* (also known as *E. herbacea)* gives excellent ground cover and is up to 30cm/12in high with a 60cm/24in spread. It has white to pink or red flowers in winter and spring. Good varieties are 'Springwood White' with white flowers, 'Myretoun Ruby' with red flowers and 'King George' with rose pink flowers. *E. cinerea* (bell heather) is also about 30cm/12in high but flowers in summer. It has purple flowers although varieties with white or almost scarlet flowers exist. A good variety is 'Purple Beauty'.

Pests and diseases Generally trouble-free.

HEATHER BED

Heathers make beautiful ground cover with other plants, or arranged in groups on their own. Choose varieties with contrasting colours and with different flowering times for all year interest.

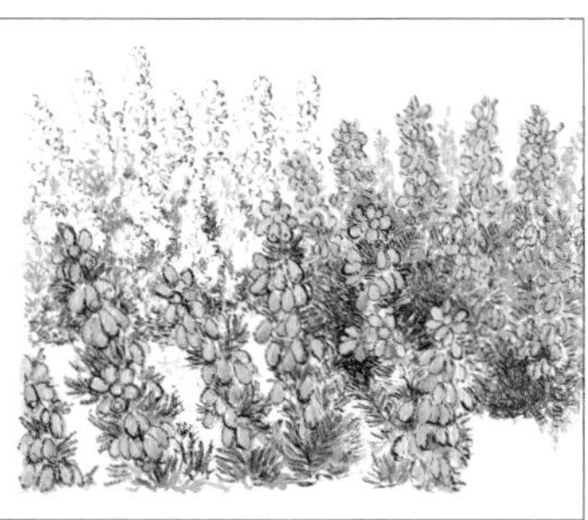

EUONYMUS/*spindle*

E. fortunei 'Emerald 'n' Gold'

A family of deciduous and evergreen trees, shrubs and ground-cover plants with insignificant flowers but very showy autumn fruits and foliage. Some forms make good hedges and all are easy to grow.

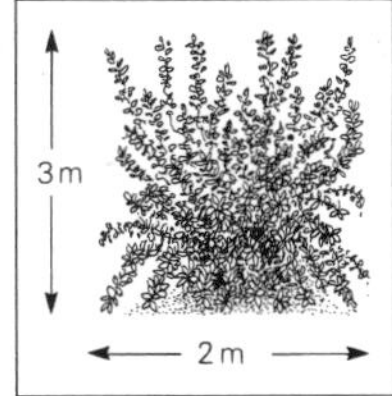

Suitable site and soil Grow in ordinary garden soil, deciduous varieties in full sun, evergreens in partial or full shade and a sheltered position.

Cultivation and care Plant deciduous species between autumn and spring and evergreens in autumn or spring. Prune hedges or shrubs in spring to desired shape. Thin out shoots of deciduous species in late winter.

AT A GLANCE

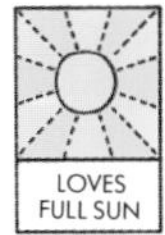

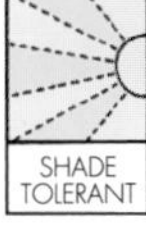

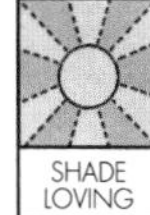

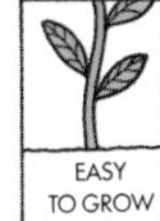

E. europaeus 'Red Cascade'

E. japonicus 'Macrophyllus Albus'

Propagation Take heel cuttings in late summer, over-winter in an equal mix of peat and sand in a cold frame. Plant out the following spring.

Recommended varieties *E. fortunei* is a hardy evergreen ground-cover plant. It has some excellent forms, including 'Emerald 'n' Gold' (bright golden variegated leaves, bronze-pink in winter), and 'Coloratus' (purple leaves in winter). *E. europaeus* is the common spindle tree with brilliant deciduous autumn foliage and rosy-red fruits (height up to 3.6m/12ft). *E. japonicus* is an evergreen, excellent for hedging and tolerant of both pollution and sea spray. It has glossy, dark green leaves and grows up to 3m/10ft. Garden forms include 'Aureopictus' or 'Aureus' (green leaves, golden centres) and 'Macrophyllus Albus' (grey-green with white edges).

Pests and diseases Aphids and scale insects.

BRIGHTENING A WINTER WALL

Use one of the brightly variegated forms of *E. fortunei* to cover a shady wall and its surrounding ground with cheerful colour in winter. This shrub grows well against a high wall.

EUPHORBIA/*spurge*

E. griffithii 'Fireglow'

This huge family of plants includes succulents, shrubs, perennials and annuals. In the garden the hardy herbaceous perennials are valuable border plants grown for their colourful bracts and foliage.

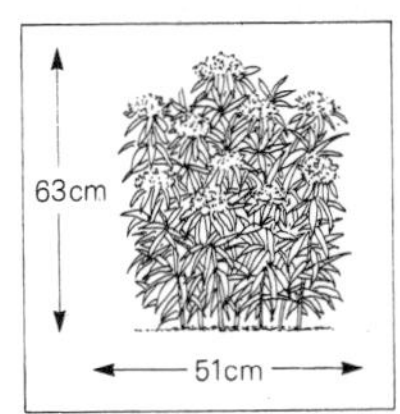

Suitable site and soil They will grow in a sunny or partially shaded site and will tolerate most soil types, but generally do best in moist yet well-drained soils.

Cultivation and care Plant from autumn to spring. No real pruning is needed but cutting back old flower stems keeps the plant bushy.

AT A GLANCE

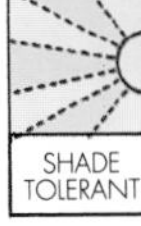

E. polychroma

E. characias wulfenii

Propagation By basal cuttings in either spring or summer or by division in early autumn or late spring. With some effort they can be grown from seed.

Recommended varieties *E. griffithii*, an excellent hardy perennial, has reddish stems up to around 60cm/2ftwith profuse dark-green leaves with red veins. The flowers bloom in summer. Best variety is 'Fireglow' with its brick-red flowerheads. *E. polychroma* is a fully hardy perennial evergreen sub-shrub with mid-green leaves and in spring sulphur-yellow flowerheads. It grows 45cm/1½ft high and wide. *E. characias wulfenii* is an upright evergreen shrub with grey-green leaves and in spring bright, greenish yellow blooms.

Pests and diseases Generally trouble-free but less than fully hardy species that are damaged by frosts might be afflicted with grey mould (botrytis).

STOP THE SAP

To prevent the irritant sap flowing from euphorbia when it is cut and used in displays, you have to scald the newly cut stems by dipping them in very hot water.

Forsythia

F. × *intermedia* 'Lynwood'

Easy to grow, hardy deciduous shrubs, forsythias really cheer up the garden with their clusters of small, bright yellow flowers, grown on long whippy shoots, between late winter and spring.

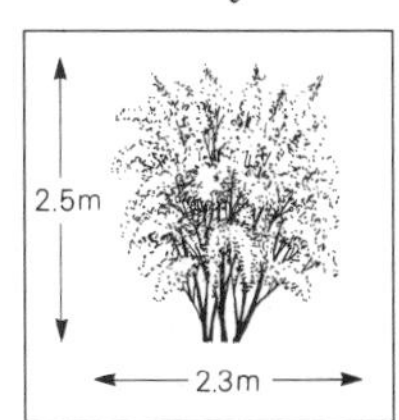

Suitable site and soil Forsythia grows happily in ordinary soil and does well in most sunny or partially shaded sites.

Cultivation and care Plant out between autumn and spring. Prune after flowering by removing stems that have just flowered and trim forsythias grown as hedges.

Propagation Can be increased easily by using cuttings in

AT A GLANCE

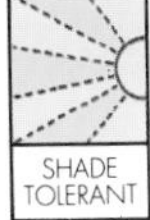

F. suspensa

F. × *intermedia* 'Spectabilis'

summer or autumn. *F. suspensa* might root itself when its branches touch the soil and can be layered in autumn.

Recommended varieties Both *F.* × *intermedia,* 'Lynwood' and 'Spectabilis' are strong-growing compact shrubs, 2.5m/8ft high by 2.3m/7½ft wide, with profuse yellow flowers. 'Spectabilis' is one of the most popular varieties and often used for hedges. Another favoured variety is 'Beatrix Farrand', whose deep yellow flowers appear from early to mid spring before fresh green leaves appear. *F. ovata* is not as big at 1.3m/4¼ft high and wide and has smaller flowers. *F. suspensa* is more slender and suitable as climber on a wall or fence where it can grow to 3m/10ft when supported.

Pests and diseases Generally trouble-free but flower buds attract birds and the plant is prone to honey-fungus.

BLOOMING GOOD

When forsythia stems have produced tight buds, cut a few from a large plant and put them indoors in a display vase. The yellow flowers will slowly come out in a warm room and really brighten it up.

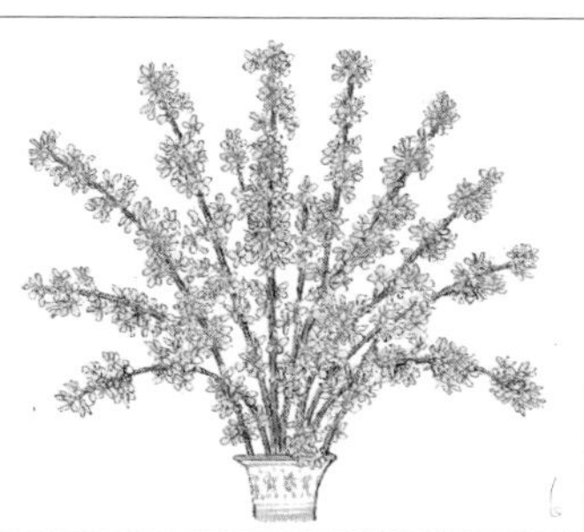

Fuchsia

F. 'Tom Thumb'

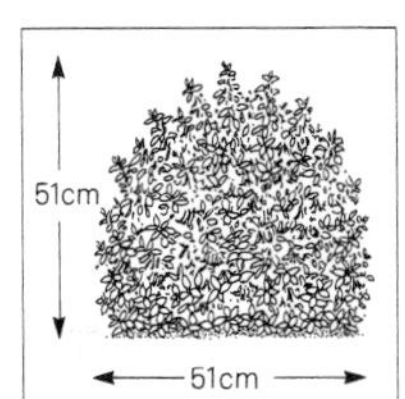

Fuchsias – evergreen and deciduous trees and shrubs – have tube-shaped hanging flowers which provide glorious colour in garden beds, tubs and hanging baskets. There is a large range of hybrids to choose from.

Suitable site and soil A sunny or semi-shaded site is best in an ordinary soil enriched with some peat or leafmould. Weeping fuchsias look good in hanging baskets, more erect ones are good in tubs or beds.

Cultivation and care Plant out in late spring or early summer. In colder parts of the country fuchsias have to be cut to ground level in late autumn or spring and the roots protected.

AT A GLANCE

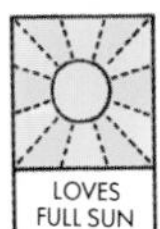

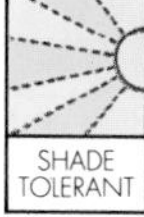

F. 'Cascade'

F. 'Ting-a-ling'

In milder regions hardy varieties can be left alone but remove any dead wood in early spring. Water often in dry spells, especially tub or basket-grown fuchsias.

Propagation Can be propagated from tip cuttings taken in early spring and also from seeds sown in spring.

Recommended varieties Some selected fuchsias are *F.* 'Tom Thumb', an erect shrub 50cm/20in high and wide with small red and dark mauve flowers and *F.* 'Lady Thumb', similar but with red and white blooms. *F.* 'Cascade', is a trailing shrub good in hanging baskets with pinky-white and deep pink flowers. *F. magellanica*, can grow to 1.8m/6ft. Other good varieties are *F.* 'Mrs Popple'; *F.* 'Ting-a-ling' which has white flowers; *F.* 'Madame Cornelissen'; and *F.* 'Brutus'.

Pests and diseases Aphids may attack plants.

PINCH YOUNG GROWTH

You can make a magnificent specimen from fuchsia grown year to year by pinching out the leading shoots in young growth. This way the plant becomes well-shaped and bushy.

GALANTHUS/*snowdrop*

G. nivalis

The delicate white flowers of the snowdrop bring life to the garden in late winter or early spring. These bulb-grown plants do well in partially shaded, cool parts of the garden such as under trees.

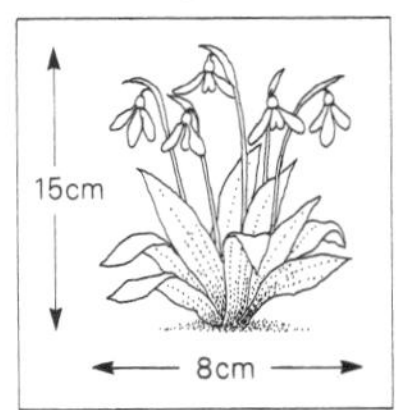

Suitable site and soil Plant in shaded areas of woodland or grass in an area where there is plenty of humus and the soil is moist.

Cultivation and care Plant bulbs 5-8cm/2-3in deep and 8-15cm/3-6in apart in late summer/early autumn. Once they have got a hold, very little care is needed but watch out for infestation by pests.

AT A GLANCE

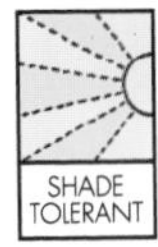

G. n 'Flore Pleno'

G. n. 'Lutescens'

Propagation Split clusters of bulbs in early spring after flowering or in early autumn. Alternatively, sow seeds from autumn to spring in pots and keep moist and in the shade.

Recommended varieties *G. nivalis* (common snowdrop) does very well growing to about 15cm/6in high with a spread of 8cm/3in. The flowers are up to 2.5cm/1in long and the inner petals have green at their tips. *G. n.* 'Flore Pleno' is a good double variety and *G. n.* 'Lutescens' is a pretty flower with yellow markings at the top of each white bloom.

Pests and diseases Can be attacked by eelworms and also by narcissus flies. Symptoms of the former are loss of colour, then rot followed by death and of the latter the death of the growing tips. In both cases the bulbs must be dug up and burnt along with any foliage. Grey mould might also be a problem; symptoms are die back and fungal growth.

SNOWDROPS IN THE BANK

Plant groups of snowdrops bulbs on a grassy bank that can be seen from within the house. Best sites are at the edge of a wooded area for a beautiful display in winter.

GENTIANA/*gentian*

G. septemfida

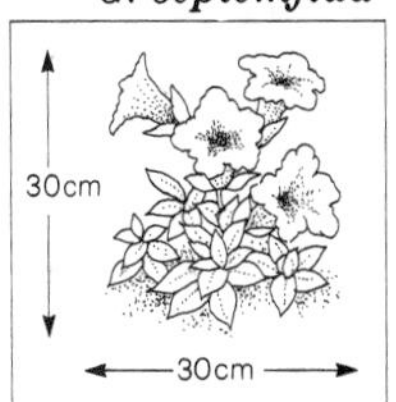

A group of hardy plants including herbaceous perennials, annuals, and biennials, many of which make a colourful contribution to rock gardens. Most garden species have blue, trumpet-like flowers.

Suitable site and soil Most prefer a humus or peat-rich, gritty, well-drained soil that is either neutral or slightly acid. Some, however, can grow on quite limy soils. Plant in sun or partial shade in a rock garden or peat bed, although large species do well in mixed borders or among shrubs.

Cultivation and care Plant out between early autumn and mid-spring. Keep the soil moist.

AT A GLANCE

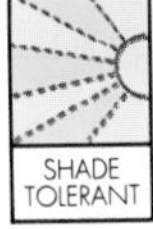

G. lutea

G. sino-ornata

Propagation Divide gentians in early spring or take cuttings from shoots in mid to late spring.

Recommended varieties *G. septemfida* reaches 30cm/12in high by 30cm/12in wide. It has groups of blue flowers in mid to late summer. *G. acaulis* forms carpets of shiny green leaves ad bears intense blue blooms in early summer. It grows 8cm/3in high by 45cm/18in across. *G. asclepiadea* (willow gentian) likes partial shade and grows 60cm/2ft high by 45cm/18in wide. Its long stems give it a 'weeping' habit by flowering time in late summer. Its flowers are blue with white markings. *G. lutea* is an erect gentian with yellow flowers in mid to late summer. It grows up to 1.5m/5ft high by 38cm/15in wide. *G. sino-ornata,* 15cm/6in high by 38cm/15in wide, has blue flowers marked with yellow in autumn.

Pests and diseases Usually no problems.

ROCK GENTIAN
Careful choice of the plants to go alongside a gentian can enhance a rock garden. Pick a red or pink-flowering plant, such as *Oxalis adenophylla*, for a complementary colour arrangement.

GERANIUM/*cranesbill*

G. psilostemon 'Bressingham Flair'

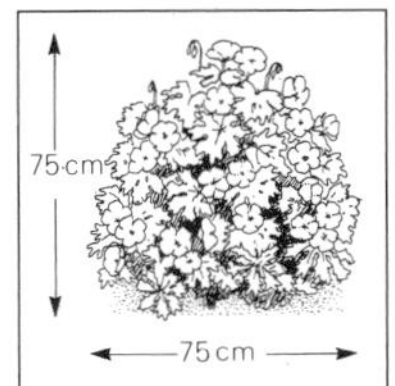

This group of hardy herbaceous perennials contains many species, and most have small, brightly coloured flowers in shades of blue, violet, pink and purple. They do well in borders, as ground cover and in rock gardens.

Suitable site and soil Generally, they will grow in most soils but do best in one that is well drained in a spot where there is plenty of sun.

Cultivation and care Plant out during autumn or spring. Tall species may need support from twigs. A second flowering and compact growth can be encouraged by cutting back old flowering stems to just above the soil.

AT A GLANCE

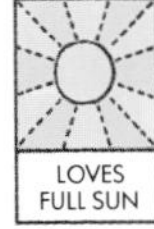

G. macrorrhizum

G. 'Johnson's Blue'

Propagation Propagate by sowing seeds in a cold frame in spring or by division in spring.

Recommended varieties *G. psilostemon*, a tall species with leaves that change colour during the year, is excellent in a sunny border. It is 75cm/2½ft high and wide and has brilliant magenta flowers with dark centres in midsummer. A good variety is 'Bressingham Flair'. *G. macrorrhizum* makes a good carpeting plant and spreads rapidly growing to 30cm/12in high. The aromatic leaves go scarlet in autumn; the flowers are either magenta or, in the variety 'Ingwersen's Variety', rose-pink. *G.* 'Johnson's Blue' is a hardy border plant with blue-mauve flowers in the middle of summer. The leaves are interestingly shaped with deep lobes and the plants grow to 40cm/16in high by 60cm/24in wide.

Pests and diseases Watch out for slug attack.

FILLING THE CRACKS

G. sanguineum not only does well in the rock garden but also fills a bare path or paved area. Plant it in soil in the crevices between slabs, where water drains and it soon covers the stones with vibrant pink.

Gladiolus

Gladiolus 'Oscar'

Superb border plants, growing from corms, with brilliantly coloured flowers in mid- and late summer. Each bloom may be as much as 10cm/4in across and they are borne on spikes 40-50cm/16-20in long.

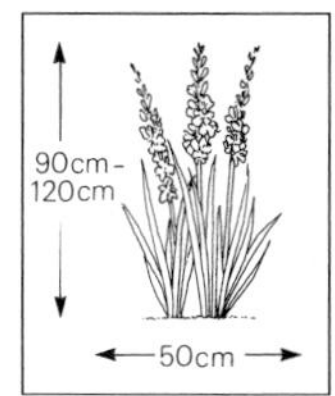

Suitable site and soil Plant in an open, sunny position. A loamy or sandy soil is best and heavy clays should be lightened with plenty of organic matter.

Cultivation and care Plant corms 10cm/4in deep and 15cm/6in apart in spring. Dress the soil with bone meal and rake in before planting. Stake all hybrid gladioli. Except for hardy types, such as *G. byzantinus*, lift the corms in autumn and dry

AT A GLANCE

G. 'Melodie'

G. byzantinus

off. Store the new, firm corms in a dry, frost-proof place.

Propagation Look for cormlets round the old corm when storing, and plant these separately in spring, 8cm/3in deep in rows in a nursery bed (a sunny corner of the garden, perhaps in the vegetable plot). Lift in autumn.

Recommended varieties For garden display, the tall, large-flowered hybrids (1.2-1.5m/4-5ft, mid-summer to early autumn) are best. For cutting, grow the butterfly types (about 1m/3ft, mid- and late summer). Hardy types include *G. byzantinus* (wine-red, 60cm/2ft, early summer).

Pests and diseases Core rot can attack corms in store. They become soft and brown. Destroy affected corms. Partly rotted corms produce abortive plants. Several fungi can occur on growing plants. If badly attacked, lift and destroy.

SOLO DISPLAY

Gladioli are not best suited to mixed planting in the garden. They look better in a separate bed, and are most attractive in groups of single colours. Choose the large-flowered showy hybrids.

HAMAMELIS/*witch hazel*

H. mollis 'Goldcrest'

These beautiful hardy shrubs flower in winter and early spring, and often have exceptional autumn leaf colour. The starry flowers are borne on the leafless branches and in many kinds are deliciously scented.

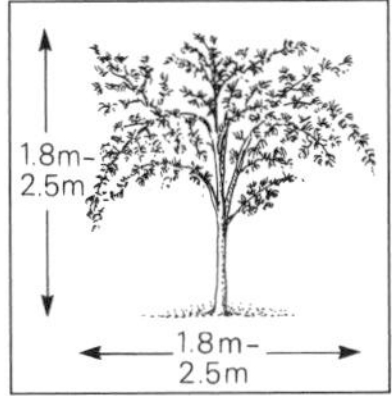

Suitable site and soil The witch hazels prefer good, deep soils, but do not like heavy clay. They are not lime haters, but chalky soils should be improved by the addition of bulky organic matter. They are happy in sun or dappled shade.

Cultivation and care Plant in autumn or spring. Before planting, dig in peat or leaf mould, as hamamelis like to root into it when young. If your shrub tends to spread and be flat-

AT A GLANCE

H. × *intermedia* 'Diane'

H. × *intermedia* 'Jelena'

topped, train up a leader by staking a branch upright until it becomes strong enough to stand on its own.

Propagation Layer in summer outdoors. Patience is needed, as it will take two years to produce well-rooted new plants. Air layering is also done in summer. Seeds sown as soon as ripe usually take over two years to germinate.

Recommended varieties *Hamamelis mollis* has large, soft, hazel-like leaves, and large, soft yellow, sweetly scented flowers in winter. 'Goldcrest' has large flowers with orange bases to the petals. *Hamamelis* × *intermedia* varieties are large-leafed, large shrubs with crimpled, sometimes scented flowers and good autumn leaf colour. 'Diane' has red flowers; 'Jelena' has coppery-orange flowers and good autumn colour.

Pests and diseases Trouble free.

GO ORGANIC

When you plant a new witch hazel, water it well and cover the soil around it with a thick layer of organic material. This will improve the soil structure and prevent evaporation.

HEDERA/*ivy*

H. helix

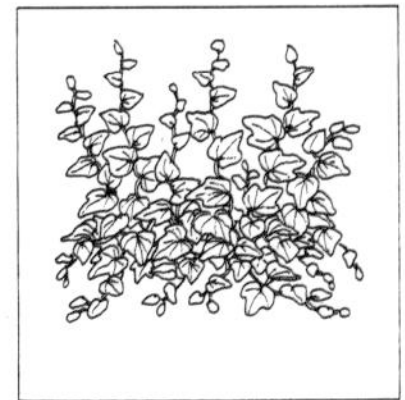

Large family of hardy and evergreen climbers with a wide range of foliage shape and colour. They can be used for ground cover, to climb supports and trail from hanging baskets or window boxes.

Suitable site and soil A sunny site is best for variegated ivy but plain ivies do well in shade or sun. Any soil.

Cultivation and care Plant new ivy from autumn to spring. Keep in bounds by pruning in spring and summer. Cut out green shoots that have reverted on variegated forms.

Propagation Take cuttings in summer. For bushy forms take

AT A GLANCE

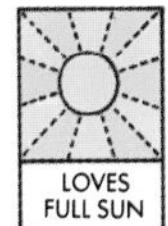

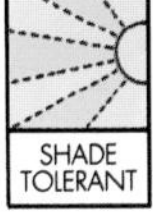

H. colchica 'Dentata Variegata'

H. helix 'Buttercup'

them from tree ivies and for climbers from juvenile runners. Plant them round the rim of a pot in a peat and sand mixture. Enclose in polythene until roots formed and grow on in pots until ready to transplant.

Recommended varieties For ground cover in shade, common ivy *H. helix* is best. For ground cover, fences and walls, use large yellow-green leafed *H. colchica* 'Dentata Variegata'. *H. helix* 'Buttercup' with all yellow leaf and 'Gold-heart' with yellow heart in summer and purple veining in winter bring all-year colour.

Pests and diseases Resistant to most pests and disease but red spider mite affects wall ivies, producing yellow spotting on leaves. Scale insects deposit sooty mould on leaves and suck sap of young shoots. In autumnal wet conditions ivy leaf spot may develop causing leaf collapse.

TRAINING IVY INTO A TOPIARY SHAPE

Use variegated or plain ivy to grow in a spiral or cone shape. Train ivy up the wire frame, winding it in and pruning into the shape as it grows.

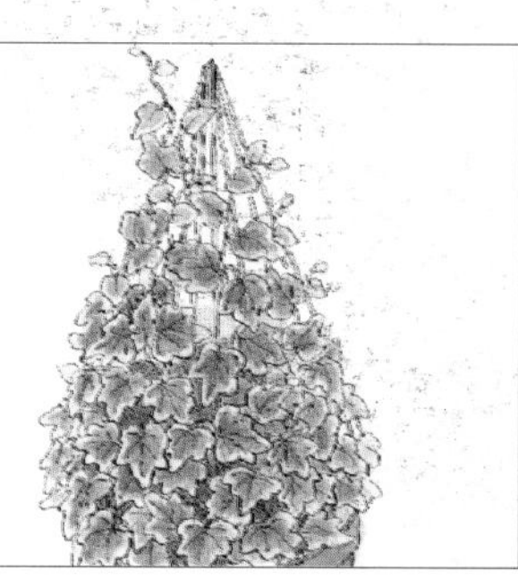

HELLEBORUS/*Christmas rose*

Helleborus niger

Hellebores are a family of delightful winter- and spring-flowering perennials. The unusual flowers can be white, cream, plum, purple and even green. They are excellent under shrubs, and mix well with early bulbs.

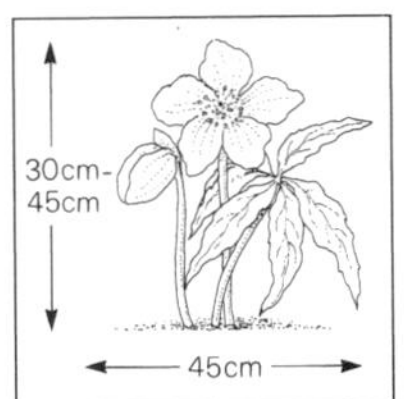

Suitable site and soil Hellebores prefer a shady position and a rich, moist – though not boggy – soil.

Cultivation and care Plant in autumn. Do not disturb the plants once they are established. Cut off the old, faded flower stems in summer. Give an occasional top-dressing of compost to keep the soil rich and moist.

AT A GLANCE

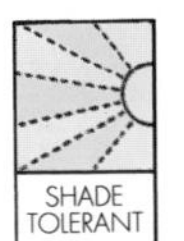

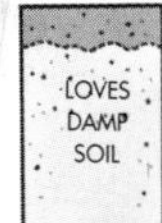

H. orientalis

H. lividus corsicus

Propagation Sow seeds in summer in a sandy soil in a cold frame. Alternatively, allow to self-seed and transplant while still small, or divide clumps after flowering.

Recommended varieties *H. niger* (Christmas rose) has leathery evergreen leaves and white, saucer-shaped flowers with gold anthers from midwinter to early spring (height 30-45cm/12-18in). *H. orientalis* (Lenten rose) is evergreen except in the coldest districts. Flowers appear in late winter and may be cream, crimson, purple, pink or white (height 30-45cm/12-18in). *H. lividus corsicus* is evergreen with greyish spiny leathery leaves. The spreading heads of flowers appear in late winter and have an unusual lime-green colour (height 60cm/24in). *H. purpurascens* is deciduous with wide saucer-shaped flowers, purple outside and green-purple inside.

Pests and diseases Leaf spot may damage the leaves.

GROUND COVER UNDER SHRUBS

The Lenten rose is an effective way of suppressing weeds under deciduous shrubs. The plants thrive in the shade offered by the shrubs and flower before the shrubs are in leaf.

HIBISCUS/*tree hollyhock*

Hibiscus trionum

This family of exotic annuals and shrubs includes some species which can only be grown in a greenhouse. The ones listed here are all hardy and renowned for their showy hollyhock-like flowers.

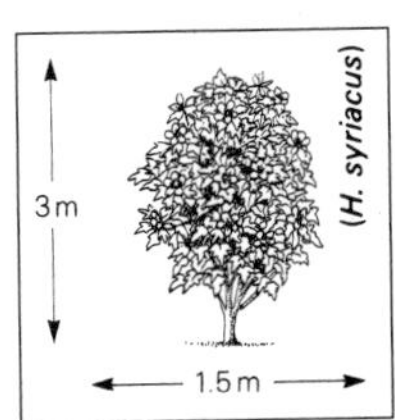

Suitable site and soil Hibiscus need an open, sunny aspect and a well-drained, humus-rich soil. They do particularly well in a sheltered spot with the protection of a wall.

Cultivation and care Sow seeds for annuals in spring where they are going to flower. Plant shrubs between autumn and spring. Remove any frost-damaged or dead wood in the spring – no other pruning is necessary.

AT A GLANCE

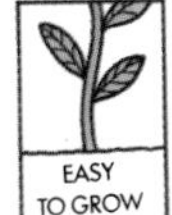

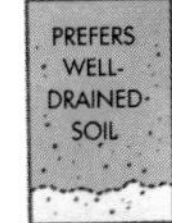

H. syriacus 'Hamabo'

H. syriacus 'Woodbridge'

Propagation Annuals often self-seed. Take heel cuttings from shrubs in summer, grow on in a potting compost in a cold frame before planting the following autumn.

Recommended varieties The annual *H. trionum* is known as the flower-of-an-hour as its creamy-white flowers with darker centres open only in the morning (height 75cm/30in). *H. syriacus* is a commonly grown shrub and is very free flowering. Recommended varieties include: 'Blue Bird' with its single, violet-blue flowers; 'Diana' has large, single white flowers; 'Hamabo' has blush-pink single flowers with a carmine eye; 'Elegantissimus' has double white flowers with a maroon eye; 'Woodbridge' has single rose-pink flowers with a carmine eye; 'Dorothy Crane' is white with a crimson eye (height 3m/10ft).

Pests and diseases Aphids may attack the new growth.

OUTSIZE FLOWERS

You can get extra-large blooms on your hibiscus shrub by pruning, as the flowers appear on the current year's growth. If you do not mind sacrificing height for show, simply cut back the old stems very hard in the spring for a display of giant flowers from midsummer through to autumn. Varieties of the popular *Hibiscus syriacus* such as 'Woodbridge' or 'Diana' are particularly good choices.

Hosta/plantain lily

Hosta fortunei

Hostas are unmistakable with their bold, luxurious leaves, often variegated. They have delicate spires of blue, lilac or white bell-like flowers in summer. They like shade and are excellent under shrubs or by water.

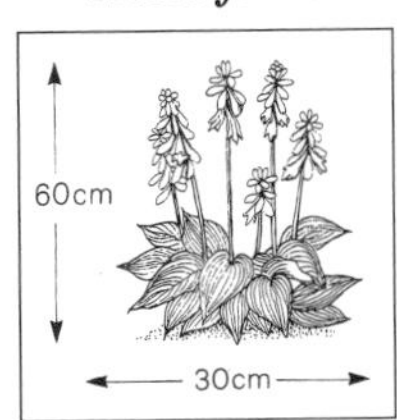

Suitable site and soil Hostas need at least partial shade and may lose their variegation if exposed to full sun. They like a rich, moisture-retentive soil with plenty of leaf mould or garden compost.

Cultivation and care Plant between autumn and spring. During any extended dry weather, water well. Mulch annually with leaf mould or garden compost.

AT A GLANCE

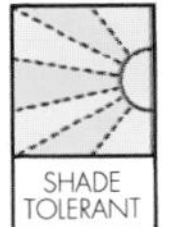

H. fortunei albopicta

H. undulata

Propagation Divide and replant in early spring.

Recommended varieties *H. fortunei* has grey-green leaves and lilac flowers appear in midsummer on stems 60cm/23in high. The form *albopicta* has lush leaves which unfurl a clear yellow with a green edge and gradually darken to two shades of green. *H. sieboldiana* forms 60cm/24in high clumps of glossy blue-green leaves and has off-white flowers. *H. crispula* has heart-shaped, dark-green leaves, edged with white and pale lilac flowers on stems 60cm/24in high. *H. plantaginea* has glossy yellow-green leaves and fragrant white flowers. It is the only hosta which likes a sunny position. *H. undulata* has wavy green leaves with white splashes and lilac flowers.

Pests and diseases Slugs can be a serious problem with hostas and may reduce the leaves to skeletons if you do not take precautions.

WATERSIDE PLANTING

Hosta's bold architectural leaves look particularly handsome reflected in water and they are ideal for planting on the shady side of the pond. Plant them in large clumps close to the water's edge.

HYACINTHUS/*hyacinth*

H. orientalis 'Delft Blue'

Hyacinths are one of the most popular of the spring bulbs with their columns of bell-shaped flowers and their heady scent. They are excellent for borders and containers – especially window boxes.

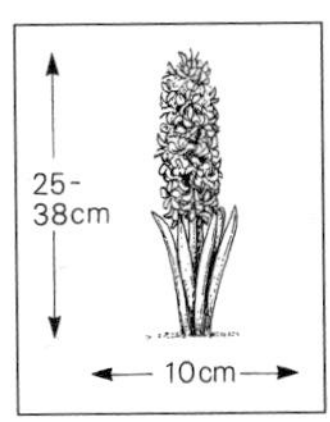

Suitable site and soil Plant in light well-drained soil and full sun in the garden or containers. For bulbs for early indoor forcing, use specially prepared bulb fibre or compost.

Cultivation and care Dead-head after flowering.

Propagation Hyacinths can be grown from seed but the bulbs can take at least three years to reach flowering size.

AT A GLANCE

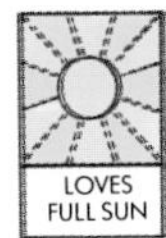

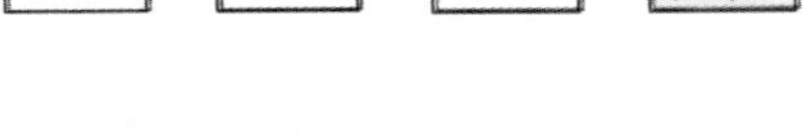

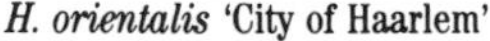
H. orientalis 'City of Haarlem'

H. orientalis 'Lady Derby'

They can also be propagated by division but this method is not always successful. It is best to buy named varieties as bulbs, which are widely available in stores and garden centres.

Recommended varieties *H. orientalis* is the original wild species, but it is the hybrids and varieties that we grow. There are many varieties, all growing to about 15-23cm/6-9in tall, but some of the best are 'Delft Blue' (porcelain blue), 'City of Haarlem' (primrose yellow), 'John Bos' (rose-red), 'L'Innocence' (white), 'Lady Derby' (shell-pink) and 'Pink Pearl' (deep pink). Cynthella hyacinths have smaller, dainty spikes, charming in small beds or window boxes. Multiflora varieties produce several slender stems of loosely spaced flowers.

Pests and diseases There are a number of fungal and physiological disorders which can affect the bulbs – apparent in poor flowers and leaves – and the bulbs should be discarded.

FORCING HYACINTHS

Buy specially prepared bulbs for early indoor flowering and plant in bowls of bulb fibre or compost in early autumn. Leave the top of the bulb above the compost and water. Make sure you keep the compost moist but not waterlogged. Leave in a cool, dark place and when 5cm/2in of growth is showing, move to a windowsill. After flowering, plant the bulbs in the garden in early spring.

Hydrangea

H. macrophylla 'Blue Wave'

These popular shrubs and climbers are well known for their distinctive flowerheads. The shrubs do best in mild areas, particularly on the coast. The climbers are hardier and will grow on shady walls.

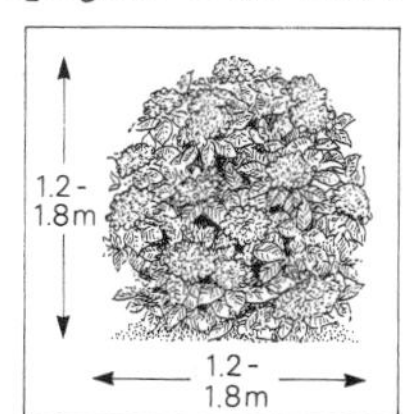

Suitable site and soil Hydrangeas like rich, moist soil and a sunny, sheltered position. Blue varieties do not produce blue flowers on alkaline soil – so dig in peat – dress with aluminium sulphate to balance. Pinks do not like acid soils – dress with ground limestone.

Cultivation and care Plant in late autumn or early spring. Give a manure mulch in spring. Dead-head after flowering.

AT A GLANCE

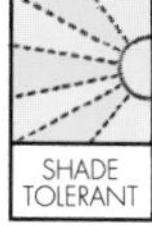

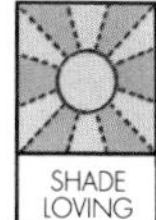

H. macrophylla 'Altona'

H. petiolaris

Propagation Take cuttings of the climbing species in early summer and of the shrubs in late summer or early autumn and grow on in a potting compost. Overwinter in a cold frame and plant out in the spring.

Recommended varieties *H. macrophylla* has two main groups – lacecaps with flat heads and hortensias with round or mopheads. Good lacecaps include: 'Blue Wave' – blue or pink; 'White Wave' – white; 'Mariesii' – rich pink or blue. Hortensias include: 'Altona' – rose-pink; 'Goliath' – rich pink or purple-blue; 'Madame Emile Moullière' – white with pink or blue centre. (Height and spread 1.2-1.8m/4-6ft). *H. petiolaris* is a vigorous climbing hydrangea with a height of up to 18m/60ft. It carries greenish-white flowers in early summer.

Pests and diseases Alkaline soil causes chlorosis, visible in yellow or almost white leaves.

CLIMBING HYDRANGEA

The climbing hydrangea is a very useful plant and one of the few flowering climbers which does best on a shady wall. It needs no support as it is self-clinging and climbs equally well on a tree.

HYPERICUM/St John's wort

H. 'Hidcote'

This family of herbaceous perennials and mostly evergreen shrubs has some easy-to-grow varieties. Its bright yellow, cup-shaped flowers appear in late summer and early autumn. Some varieties bear simultaneous fruits.

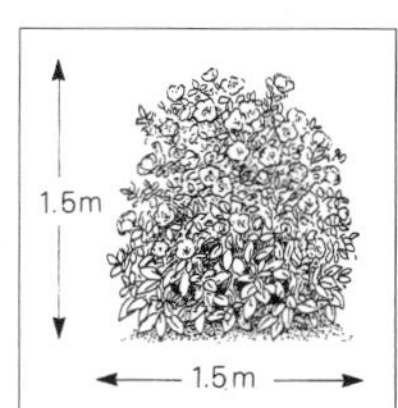

Suitable site and soil St John's wort will grow in almost all well-drained soils and, though many varieties will tolerate shade, flowering is best in full sun.

Cultivation and care Prune the larger shrubs by about a third in spring, using shears, and cut out any old or damaged stems. *H. calycinum* should be clipped back hard, pruning it down almost to ground level.

AT A GLANCE

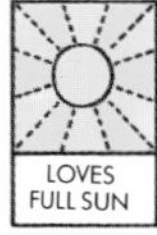

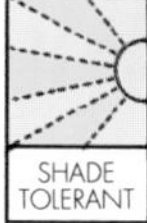

H. × *moseranum* 'Tricolor'

H. × *inodorum* 'Elstead'

Propagation Take cuttings with a heel in summer of shrubs, in spring of herbaceous plants, and grow on in a cold frame. Transplant to flowering positions the following spring.

Recommended varieties *H.* 'Hidcote' is one of the most spectacular and popular of the shrubs. It has large abundant golden flowers from midsummer to late autumn (height 1.5m/5ft). *H.* × *moseranum* has arching reddish stems and the flowers have red anthers. *H.* × *m.* 'Tricolor' is a dwarf shrub with variegated pink, white and green leaves. *H. inodorum* has pale yellow flowers and fruits. The form 'Elstead' has brilliant salmon-red fruits at the same time as the flowers. *H. calycinum* (rose of Sharon) is a small shrub (30-45cm/12-18in) which grows in dry and shady places. *H. olympicum* is a good rock garden plant with grey-green leaves.

Pests and diseases Rust may appear as spots on the leaves.

BERRY ARRANGEMENTS

H. × *inodorum* and its form 'Elstead' both have brilliant red or pink fruits which appear at the same time as their golden flowers. The berrying branches look lovely and last well in flower arrangements.

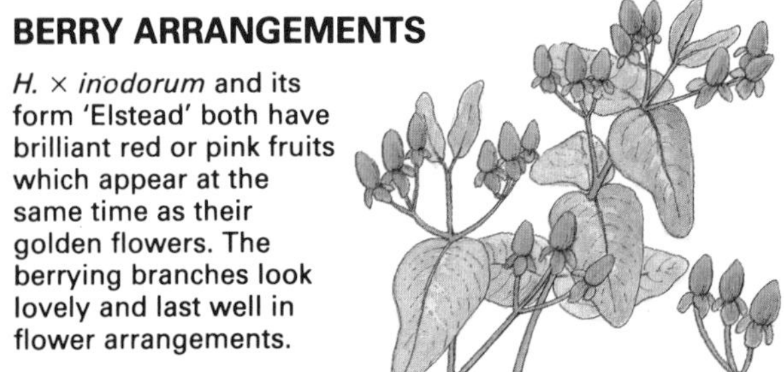

ILEX/*holly*

I. aquifolium 'Madame Briot'

Known world-wide for glossy, prickly leaves and the gleaming berries of common holly, this group of trees and shrubs can be tender or hardy, deciduous or evergreen, with a range of leaf variegation and berry colour.

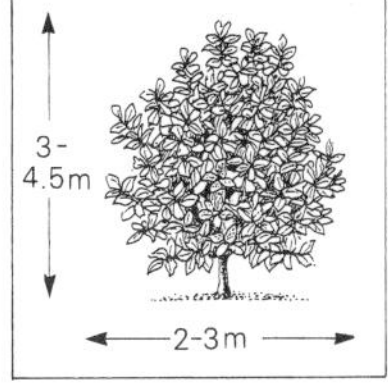

Suitable site and soil Most grow well in sun or shade (full sun for variegated hollies). Well-drained garden soil is best.

Cultivation and care Plant in autumn or spring. Water well until established, protect young plants from winter winds with hessian or netscreens. Prune holly hedges in spring, specimen trees to shape in summer, and cut out completely shoots that revert to green on variegated forms.

AT A GLANCE

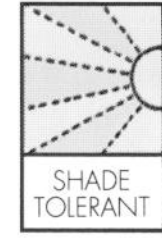

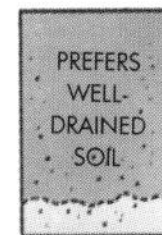

I.a. 'Pyramidalis Fructuluteo'

I.a. 'Silver Queen'

Propagation In summer take heeled cuttings and over-winter in a cold frame. Grow on in spring in nursery beds for up to two years before planting out permanently.

Recommended varieties For yellow berries, *Ilex aquifolium* 'Pyramidalis Fructuluteo'; orange berries, 'Amber'. For silver-edged green leaves and red berries use 'Handsworth New Silver'. 'Madame Briot' has gold-edged green leaves and scarlet berries. Grow it with male holly 'Silver Queen' with silver-edged spiny leaves. Prickliest holly for a hedge is 'Ferox'. Use variegated hollies as highlights for winter colour; dark green holly makes a good background for other shrubs.

Pests and diseases Unsightly marks on leaves can be caused by holly leaf miner. Caterpillars of the holly blue butterfly feed on flowers and young foliage in spring. Leaf spot marks leaves.

BERRIES FOR CHRISTMAS

Almost all hollies are unisexual, with the result that the berries are borne only on female plants. Therefore, for berry production in winter, male and female trees are necessary, although *Ilex aquifolium* 'J.C. van Tol' and 'Pyramidalis' are self-fertile. Attractive red, yellow or black berries are produced after spring fertilization of tiny white flowers on well-established female plants.

IMPATIENS/*busy Lizzie*

Impatiens 'Imp Strain'

Busy Lizzies are well known as houseplants and indoors will often flower almost continually. There are, though, varieties which are good for outdoor bedding; they are not hardy and should be treated as annuals.

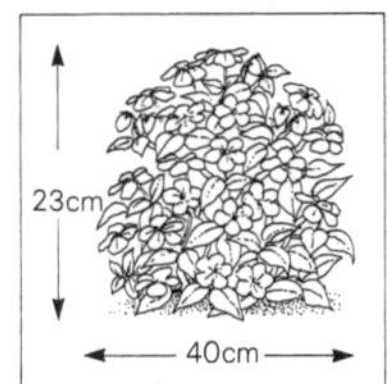

Suitable site and soil Grow in full sun or partial shade in a sheltered spot in the border. Busy Lizzies are particularly good for window boxes and other containers.

Cultivation and care Keep well watered, especially plants grown in containers. If young plants start to get too 'leggy', pinch out the tips.

AT A GLANCE

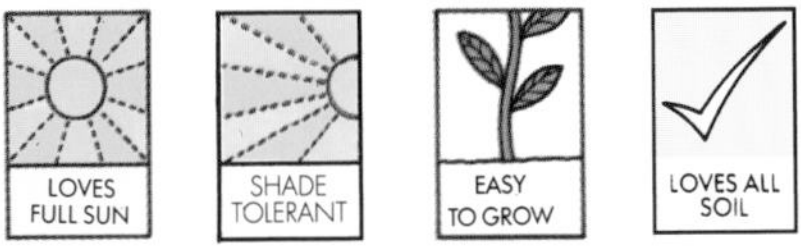

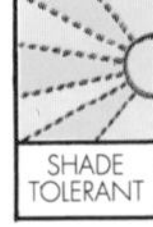

I. 'Zig Zag'

I. balsamina

Propagation Sow seeds in spring, and prick off into seed trays or individual pots. Do not plant out until danger of frost has passed. For indoor plants, cuttings can be taken, preferably in summer or early autumn. They will root in water.

Recommended varieties Hybrid varieties of *Impatiens walleriana* are best for outdoor bedding and flower continuously from early summer to autumn. 'Novette' (height 10cm/4in) and 'Florette' (15cm/6in) are good for edgings and fronts of borders. 'Imp Strain' (23cm/9in) is single coloured with white, pink, scarlet or orange flowers; 'Zig Zag' (15cm/6in) has large flowers with a white stripe. *I. balsamina* (60cm/2ft) is a tender annual with large pink flowers. *I. biflora* is a hardy annual with orange flowers from midsummer to autumn.

Pests and diseases Busy Lizzies attract aphids.

EASY PROPAGATION

Busy Lizzies are extremely easy to propagate from stem cuttings and children often find the speedy results exciting. Simply put a 7.5-10cm/3-4in cutting in water.

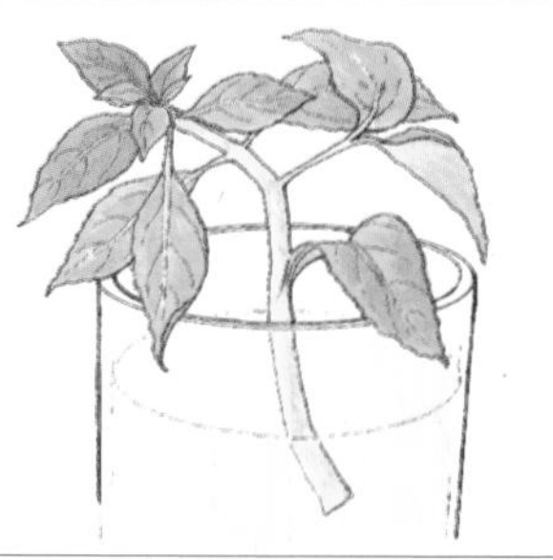

Iris

Iris 'Dancer's Veil'

This huge family of distinctive, exquisite flowers is divided into four main groups: bearded iris (with hairy lower petals); beardless iris (smooth petals); crested iris; and bulbous iris (grown from bulbs not rhizomes).

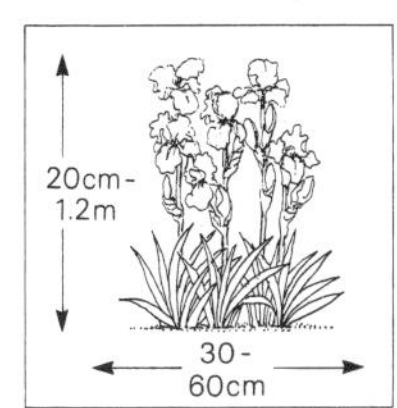

Suitable site and soil There are iris suitable for most kinds of soil and site and all have their own individual requirements, so check with the nursery before planting.

Cultivation and care Taller varieties need staking. Many need specific feeding, so again check with the nursery or a gardening reference book.

AT A GLANCE

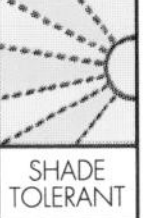

I. 'White Swirl'

I. reticulata 'Harmony'

Propagation Bulbous iris should be divided in the autumn. Rhizomes should generally be divided and replanted immediately after flowering.

Recommended varieties Bearded iris: the hybrids offer a wide range of colour – creams, pinks, browns, and blues – and a heady scent. There are all sizes from dwarfs (20cm/8in) up to 90-120cm/3-4ft, including 'Dancer's Veil', white with purple streaks, and 'Esther Fay', an apricot-pink. Beardless iris: the hybrids include 'Cambridge' pale blue; 'White Swirl' pure white, as well as the water irises such as *L. laevigata* and *I. pseudacorus*, which grows in water up to 45cm/18in deep and has bright yellow flowers. Crested iris are generally too tender for the garden. Bulbous iris include the rockery variety, *I. reticulata,* which flowers in early spring.

Pests and diseases Aphids and fungal disorders can occur.

THE WOODLAND IRIS

Iris foetidissima is known as stinking iris – though its smell is only noticeable when bruised. It is a very useful plant as it grows in complete shade (it is native to woodland) and has striking bright orange seeds which appear in the autumn and can last all winter.

The flower stems can be picked and hung upside down to dry. They can then be used in winter floral decorations.

JASMINUM/*jasmine*

Jasminum officinale

These deservedly popular shrubs and climbers are loved for their pretty white or yellow flowers and their rich, heavy scent. They are easy to grow and should be grown around a doorway or close to a seating area.

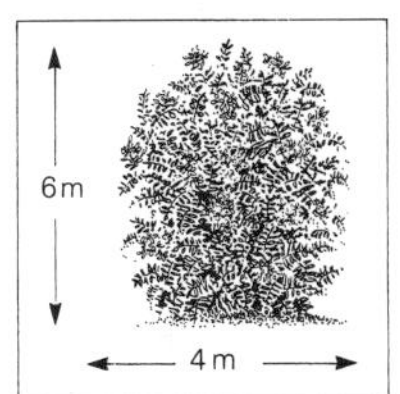

Suitable site and soil Jasmine thrives in an ordinary well-drained soil. Young plants need some protection in winter. *J. nudiflorum* will tolerate total shade but does not like morning sun which can damage the flowers. *J. officinale* prefers sun or partial shade.

Cultivation and care Plant between autumn and spring. Prune *J. nudiflorum* flowering shoots back close to the base

AT A GLANCE

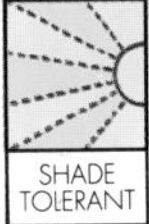

J.o. 'Aureo-variegatum'

J. nudiflorum

after flowering but do not cut the whole plant back into the old wood. Thin out *J. officinale* after flowering, but do not cut back hard. Tie the shoots into the supports with garden twine leaving room for movement and growth.

Propagation Take cuttings in late summer or autumn and overwinter under glass.

Recommended varieties *J. officinale* is the common white jasmine which flowers from early summer to autumn. It is a vigorous climber with tiny white flowers and delicate mid-green leaves. 'Aureo-variegatum' (or 'Aureum') has leaves blotched with creamy-yellow. *J. nudiflorum* flowers in winter and carries golden-yellow flowers on bare branches, but lacks the fragrance of summer flowering species.

Pests and diseases Generally trouble-free.

A SCENTED ARBOUR

The scent of jasmine is so special, it deserves to be the focus of a summer arbour. A rustic seat and trellis are perfect, especially if grown with a scented rose.

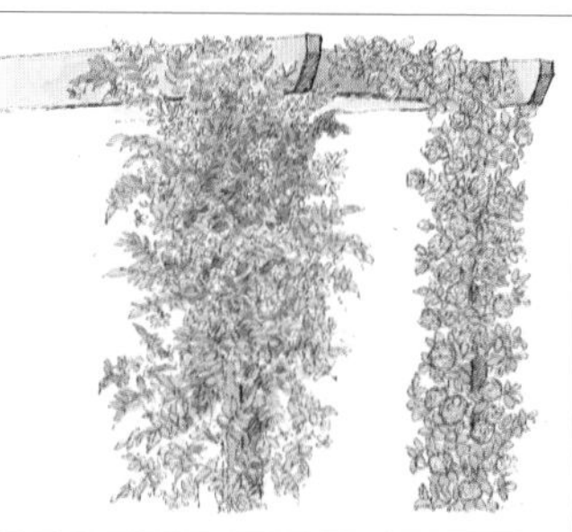

KNIPHOFIA/*red hot poker/torch lily*

Kniphofia galpinii

A family of hardy herbaceous perennials with distinctive spikes of closely set, tubular flowers in burning colours of reds, oranges and golds, which appear from early summer to late autumn.

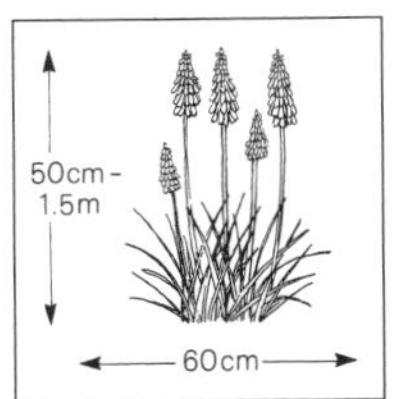

Suitable site and soil Set the plants deeply in the ground 60cm/2ft apart in well-drained garden soil and full sun. In cold areas, cover with a cloche or a blanket of straw or bracken during winter.

Cultivation and care Plant in autumn or spring. In early summer apply a light fertilizer. Cut off faded flower stems in autumn. No staking required.

AT A GLANCE

K.u. 'Bees' Lemon'

K. caulescens

Propagation Divide and replant in spring, taking care to disturb the roots as little as possible. Alternatively, sow named seeds from a nursery in drills outdoors 12mm/½in deep in spring and transplant to their flowering positions a year later. Self-sown seedlings are rarely true to the parent plant.

Recommended varieties *K. galpinii* has drooping, flame-coloured flowers on slender stems and grassy clumps of leaves (height 50cm/20in). 'Bressingham Torch' is a taller hybrid (90cm/3ft). *K. uvaria* has various forms which can grow up to 1.5m/5ft, including 'Bees' Lemon' with lemon-yellow flowers (105cm/3½ft); 'Maid of Orleans' (75cm/2½ft) with creamy-white flowers; 'Samuel's Sensation' (1.5m/5ft) bright scarlet. *K. caulescens* has all-year-round foliage of long grey leaves. The flower buds are a pinkish-red and later fade to cream.

Pests and diseases Generally trouble free.

FLOWERS FOR ARRANGEMENTS

Red hot pokers are a must for the flower arranger's garden. Arrange the hottest colours with the cooling feathery flowers of *Alchemilla mollis* for a stunning display.

LATHYRUS/*sweet pea*

Lathyrus 'Air Warden'

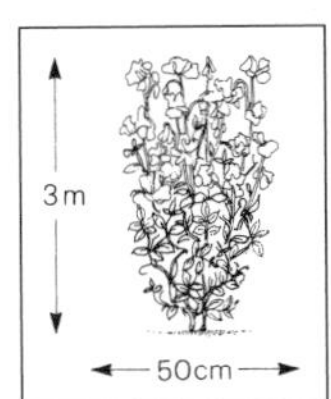

Hardy annuals and herbaceous perennials that are enjoyed for their colourful and sometimes fragrant, pea-like flowers. Most are climbing plants that cling with tendrils to netting, trellis and cane supports.

Suitable site and soil Plant in fertile, well-drained garden soil in full sun, with cane or netting support if necessary.

Cultivation and care Pick or dead-head to encourage flowering. Cut back perennials to ground level in autumn.

Propagation Sow annuals in pots to overwinter in cold frames or direct in spring. Sow perennials into pots in a cold

AT A GLANCE

L. odoratus 'Bijou'

L. latifolius

frame in spring for planting out in autumn. If necessary allow seed to sprout and soak it overnight before sowing.

Recommended varieties Annual sweet pea (*L. odoratus*) is the most widely grown and there are hundreds of garden varieties. Spencer varieties are the tallest, reaching 3m/10ft. They flower in summer with several blooms per stem. 'Princess Elizabeth' is orange-pink; 'Air Warden' is scarlet. Lower-growing, self-supporting sweet peas include 'Bijou', 'Knee-Hi' and 'Little Sweetheart'. Everlasting sweet pea (*L. latifolius*) comes in white and pink forms. Also perennial is *L. vernus*, a non-climbing species that spreads about 30cm/12in. It suits a sunny rockery or patio container.

Pests and diseases Slugs destroy seedlings in winter and early spring. Plants may be affected by mildews and moulds. In a wet spring grey mould may rot buds and flowers.

SWEET PEA HEDGE
Use tall-growing sweet peas as a curtain of colour. Dig a trench and add well-rotted compost. Erect a netting support fixed to tall canes. Set plants in trench and pinch out when three pairs of leaves appear.

LAVANDULA/*lavender*

Lavandula angustifolia 'Hidcote'

These popular, mostly hardy, evergreen shrubs are loved for their scented purple, white or green flowers. They are useful as low growing hedges, edging and can be pruned into topiary shapes in time.

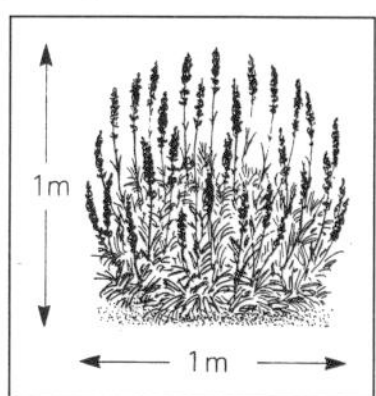

Suitable site and soil Plant in an open and sunny position in a sandy soil with good drainage and lime.

Cultivation and care Remove flowering stalks and prune lightly in autumn, but never cut back into old wood.

Propagation Take 10-20cm/4-8in ripe stem cuttings in autumn and root them in sand and peat in trays. Overwinter in a

AT A GLANCE

L. angustifolia 'Nana Alba'

L. stoechas

cold frame and plant out in spring. Sow seed in autumn to plant out in spring, but may not come true from seed.

Recommended varieties For a hedge *L. angustifolia* (English lavender) responds to hard pruning. *L. stoechas* (French lavender) needs a sheltered site. Its flowers have several purple tassels and resemble tiny woven baskets. Similar, but with green flowers, is *L. stoechas* 'Viridis'. For low-growing hedges choose *L. angustifolia* 'Hidcote', 'Twickle' and 'Folgate' with grey-green leaves. 'Munstead' has green leaves and flowers early. For pinkish flowers try 'Loddon Pink' and for a white flower, 'Nana Alba'. *L. lanata* (woolly lavender) with silvery leaves needs shelter.

Pests and diseases Grey mould affects if very wet. Young shoots may die back after severe frost damage.

DRYING LAVENDER FLOWERS

Pick flowers just as they begin to open. Cut long stems. Suspend the bunches upside down from a bamboo cane in a dry, dark and airy room. Crumble the flowers into sachets.

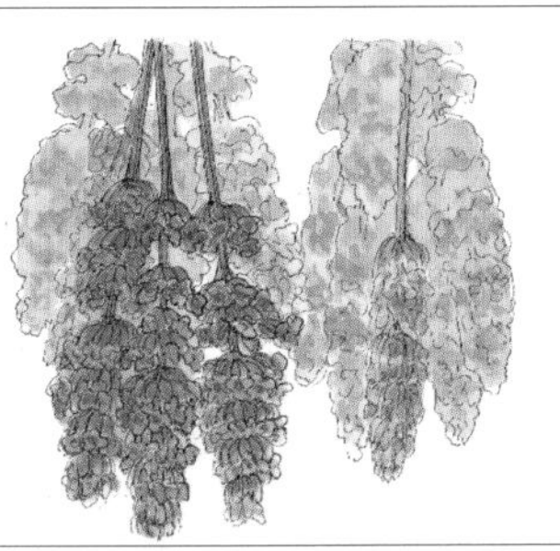

Ligustrum/*privet*

Ligustrum vulgare

These hardy, mostly evergreen shrubs are well-known as neatly-cut front garden hedges. They respond well to hard pruning and can be clipped into fanciful topiary shapes. Their flowers have a heavy, unpleasant scent.

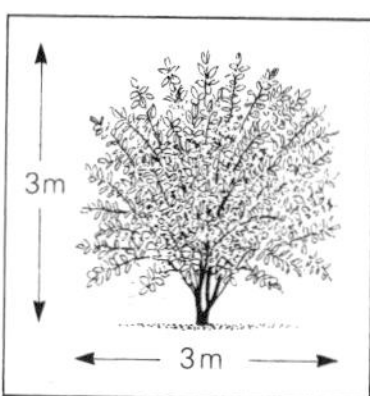

Suitable site and soil Privet thrives in any soil and in sun or shade, although sun is best for variegated forms.

Cultivation and care Plant young shrubs between autumn and spring. Prune hedges in hard spring and autumn.

Propagation Take semi-ripe cuttings in summer and overwinter them in a cold frame; plant out the following autumn.

AT A GLANCE

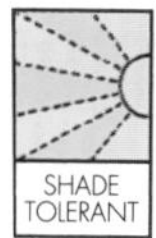

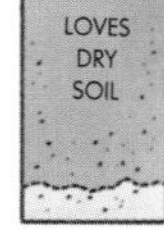

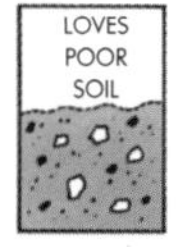

L. ovalifolium 'Aureum'

L. japonicum 'Macrophyllum'

Recommended varieties *Ligustrum vulgare* (common privet), a traditional hedge plant, is semi-evergreen. 'Aureum' has golden-yellow leaves. Both have white flowers with heavy perfume. For glossy green leaves, *L. japonicum* (Japanese privet) is best. It grows to 3m/10ft. Often grown as a specimen shrub, *L. lucidum* 'Excelsum Superbum' has creamy-yellow leaf markings, but should not be cut back. *L. ovalifolium* suits hedging best as it has larger leaves and a good branching structure. There are two variegated forms: 'Aureum' with green centre and yellow edges and 'Argenteum' with creamy-white edges. Both varieties may lose their leaves in very severe weather conditions.

Pests and diseases Leaf miner causes dark marks on leaves and premature leaf fall is caused by thrip damage. It is important to note that an entire hedge can be killed by a quick spread of honey fungus.

PRIVET TOPIARY

Birds, aeroplanes and formal shapes are popular subjects for topiary work. Allow long leading shoots to develop in your chosen shape. Reduce those that do not fit the scheme and clip often.

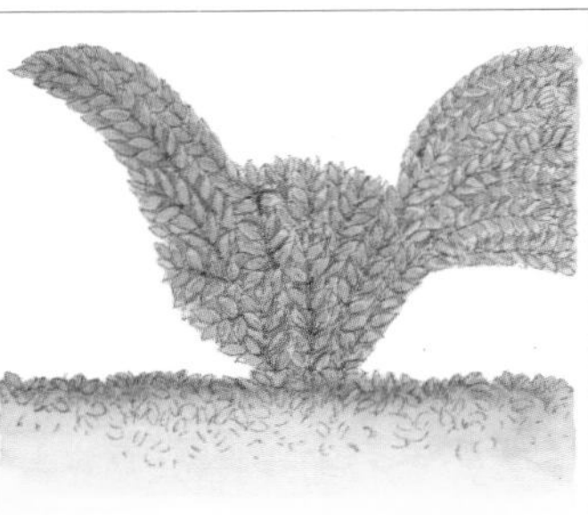

LILIUM/*lily*

Lilium candidum

Summer-flowering, lilies are mostly hardy, bulbous plants grown for their beautiful and varied blooms. There are some 80 species with numerous hybrids. Tall varieties suit wide mixed borders; dwarf ones suit rockeries.

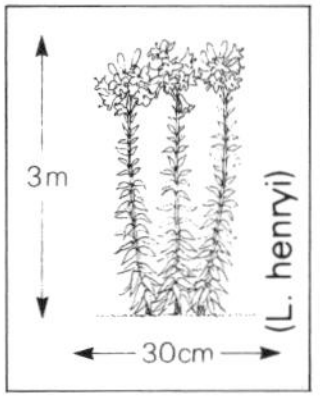

Suitable site and soil Plant in a well-drained sunny site. As they grow, other plants will provide dappled shade. Modern lily hybrids are tolerant of most soils.

Cultivation and care Plant from late summer to spring. Cover with at least 15cm/6in soil. Water well and regularly in summer and apply a liquid feed. Stake tall specimens in spring. Remove faded blooms to encourage flowering.

AT A GLANCE

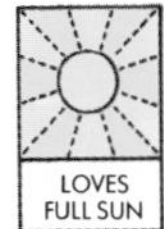

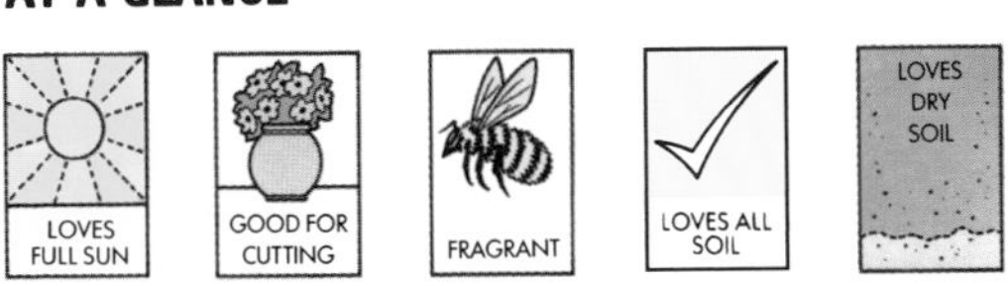

L. henryi

L. 'Imperial Crimson'

Propagation Increase from seed, bulb divisions, bulb scales or bulbils. All require special procedures.

Recommended varieties *L. candidum* (Madonna lily) is lime tolerant. Its pure white, trumpet-shaped flowers are fragrant. *L. henryi* (Henry's lily) grows to 3m/10ft with orange flowers. Its petals curve back in turk's cap shape. *L. lancifolium* (syn. *L.tigrinum*) (tiger lily) grows to 1.5m/5ft and produces orange turk's cap flowers with brown spotting. *L. longiflorum* (Easter lily) grows to a modest 1m/3ft and has white, fragrant, trumpet-shaped flowers in summer but needs winter protection. *L.* 'Imperial Crimson' has flattish shaped flowers with pink spotting on the petals; *'Connecticut King'* has open, upward-facing yellow flowers.

Pests and diseases Lily beetle larvae damage leaves, stems and buds. Botrytis causes leaf and stem damage.

NEW PLANTS FROM SCALES

When plants are dormant, remove healthy scales from bulbs. Plant in trays of peat and sand in a cold frame. Tiny new bulbs form at base of scales. Pot and grow on in a frame for three years.

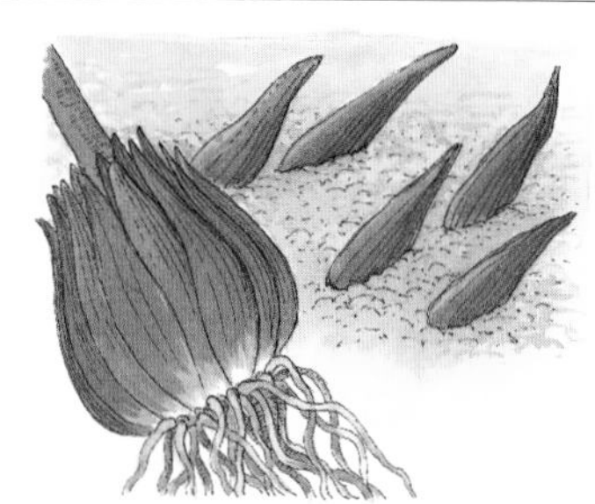

LOBELIA

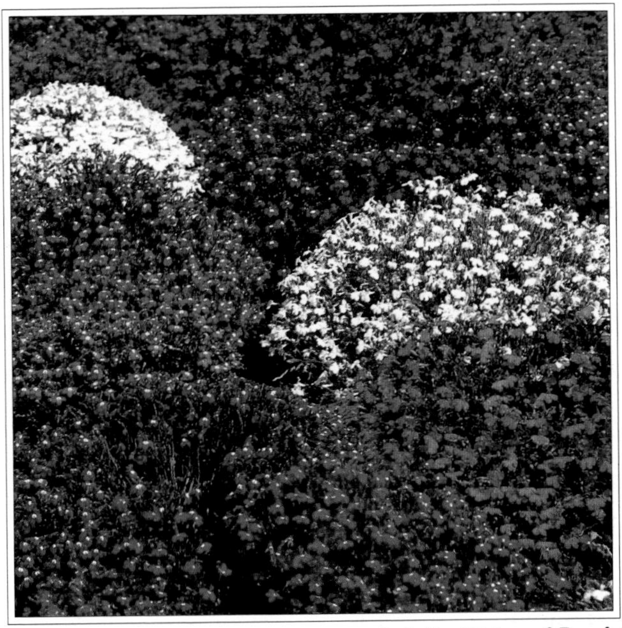

Lobelia 'String of Pearls'

Superb in hanging baskets, as edging and in herbaceous borders, the lobelia group consists of tender, half and fully hardy sub-shrubs, herbaceous perennials and annuals. Their flowers are white, red or blue.

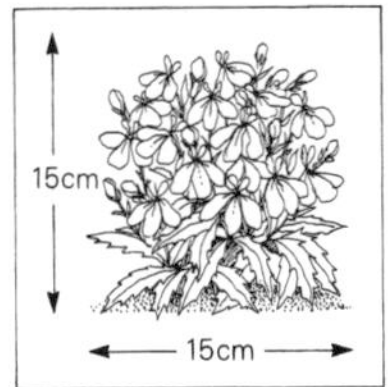

Suitable site and soil A partially shaded position where the soil is deep, well-manured and moist is best.

Cultivation and care Plant out tender species in late spring, others in early spring. Keep the soil moist especially in tubs.

Propagation Can be grown from seeds, and larger herbaceous plants can be divided in early spring.

AT A GLANCE

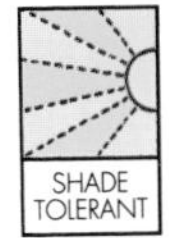

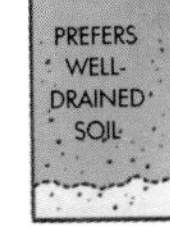

L. 'Crystal Palace'

L. cardinalis

Recommended varieties Varieties of perennial *L. erinus,* either in pendulous form for hanging baskets or tubs, or as compact bedding plants for border edges, are grown as annuals and flower profusely from spring until frost stops them. They grow to about 15cm/6in; mixed colour varieties such as 'String of Pearls' and 'Colour Cascade' are popular. Good single colour varieties are: 'Crystal Palace' – deep blue flowers and bronze leaves; the slow-growing, pendulous 'Sapphire' – blue flowers with white centres. Different to the dwarf bedding varieties are the erect, clump forming perennials. Recommended are *L.cardinalis* growing to 75cm/2½ft with red flowers in the middle summer months and *L. siphilitica* growing to 90cm/3ft with long sprays of blue flowers from late summer to mid autumn. *L. siphilitica* flourishes in damp, heavy soil.

Pests and diseases May suffer from fungal diseases.

IMPERIAL BORDER

Plant *L. cardinalis* along with *Geranium psilostemon*, purple delphiniums and campanulas, fuchsias, clematis, heliotrope and red lychins for a royal display of red and purple in a border.

LONICERA/*honeysuckle*

L. periclymenum 'Belgica'

A medium-sized group of evergreen, semi-evergreen and deciduous shrubs and climbers with woody stems that are grown for their beautiful, often fragrant, flowers. They can be trained, grown in tubs or as hedges.

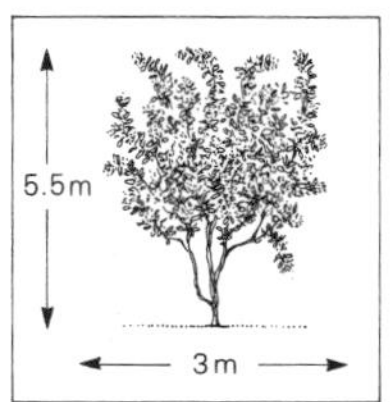

Suitable site and soil They do well in any reasonably fertile, well-drained soil in sun or semi-shade.

Cultivation and care Plants might need pruning after flowering to remove unwanted growth; hedges need trimming to remain bushy. Spring is the time to plant out evergreen climbers while deciduous or shrubby plants are best planted out in autumn or winter.

AT A GLANCE

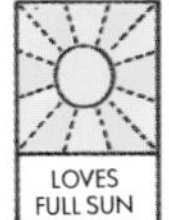

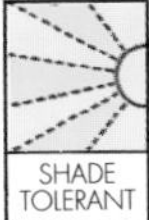

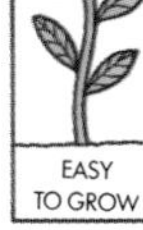

L. japonica 'Aureoreticulata'

L. nitida 'Baggesen's Gold'

Propagation Climbers are best layered in spring or autumn; shrubby types are increased from cuttings in summer.

Recommended varieties The excellent deciduous climber *L. periclymenum* 'Belgica' (or early Dutch) grows up to 5.5m/18ft and has deep, almost purple-red and yellow flowers produced in early summer. Another good climber is *L. japonica* growing up to 9m/30ft, an evergreen with 'furry' leaves and fragrant pale yellow or white flowers produced from mid summer to autumn; a good variety is *L. japonica* 'Aureoreticulata' with yellow-veined leaves. A fine shrubby honeysuckle is *L. fragrantissima* growing to about 1.8m/6ft; it has very sweet-smelling, small creamy-white flowers produced in winter and early spring. *L. nitida* is good for hedges; *L.n.* 'Baggesen's Gold' is attractive, with tiny, bright yellow leaves.

Pests and diseases Prone to aphids and fungal infections.

HONEYSUCKLE HEDGE

L. nitida is densely branched and has small round leaves. It makes an attractive hedge up to about 1.5m/5ft. Plant about 30cm/1ft apart in moderately good soil and keep well trimmed.

LUNARIA/*honesty, moonwort*

Lunaria annua

A small group of biennial and perennial herbaceous plants grown for their fragrant small flowers. They are famous, however, for their seed pods which make an unusual display in dried plant arrangements.

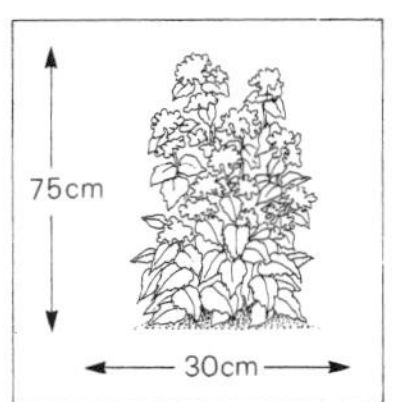

Suitable site and soil They do best in well-drained soil in partial shade. A good site is light, dry soil under trees.

Cultivation and care Plant out those grown from seedlings in autumn. Once established it will self-seed prolifically.

Propagation The biennials are grown from seed only, while the perennials can also be divided in spring.

AT A GLANCE

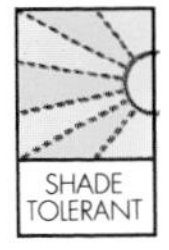

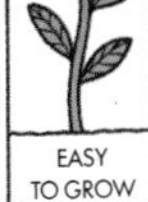

L. annua

L. rediviva

Recommended varieties *L. annua* (also known as *L. biennis*) is best known for its seed pods which are transparent, parchment-like, silvery disks about 3cm/1in across but this biennial also has attractive clusters of small, fragrant purple flowers in late spring and the mid-green leaves are toothed and heart-shaped; it grows to 75cm/2½ft high by about 30cm/1ft across. There is a white-flowered form *L.a.* 'Alba' and one with variegated leaves *L.a.* 'Variegata'. Another honesty is *L. rediviva* which grows up to 1m/3½ft. It is a bush-like perennial with small, white fragrant flowers in spring. This plant also produces silvery seed pods which are useful for dried flower displays.

Pests and diseases Usually no problems from pests but they are prone to fungal diseases including club root and white blister. There is also a viral disease which can deform the flowers and cause them to be streaked.

PODS ON DISPLAY
The dried seed pods of *L. annua* – gleaming and shimmering – make one of the most distinctive elements in any dried flower display. Be sure to pick them in good time to avoid autumn weather damage.

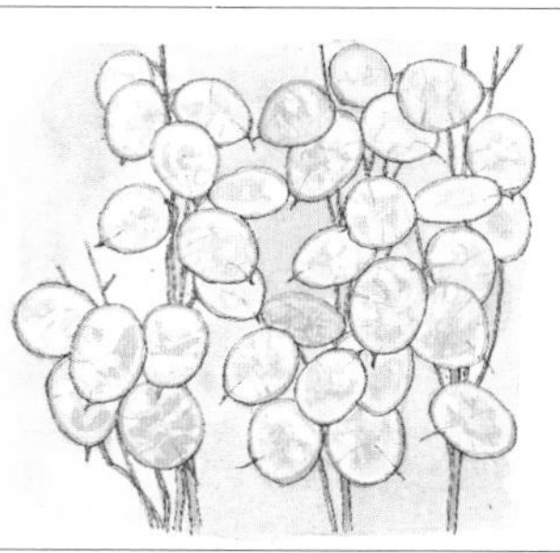

LUPINUS/*lupin*

Lupinus (Russell hybrids)

This group of sub-shrubs, herbaceous perennials and annuals has hardy and half-hardy members grown for their impressive, spire-shaped displays of small flowers in shades from white, cream and yellow, blue and red.

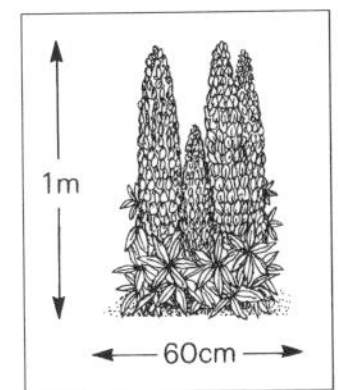

Suitable site and soil Pick a sunny position and a soil that is light, sandy, porous and perhaps slightly acid, not alkaline. They look good planted in groups in borders where their imposing display of flowers can stand out.

Cultivation and care Plant out from autumn to spring. Take off faded part of flowering stems to promote flowering and cut back flowering stems after flowering.

AT A GLANCE

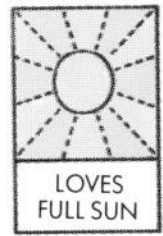

L. 'Monarch Russell'

L. arboreus

Propagation Sow fresh seeds of annuals in autumn or take cuttings from named varieties in late spring. Raise *L. arboreus* from seed or semi-ripe cuttings in mid summer.

Recommended varieties Most lupins grown are hybrid varieties of what is known as the 'Russell Strain' (crosses between *L. polyphyllus, L. arboreus* and other species). The usual height for these is about 1m/3ft and many have petals in different colours; flowers are produced in late spring and summer. They are often sold as mixed-colour seed selections with names such as 'Russell Mixed' or 'Band of Nobles'. *L. arboreus* (tree lupin) is often grown and is a large, almost shrubby perennial with a semi-permanent, woody framework. The yellow, fragrant flowers are borne in early summer.

Pests and diseases Usually no trouble from pests but perennials are prone to viral and fungal ailments.

CUT LUPINS

With their tall, dense racemes of flowers, lupins make striking plants for large displays. They can be used in the display as both vertical elements and, in short-lived centrepiece displays, horizontally.

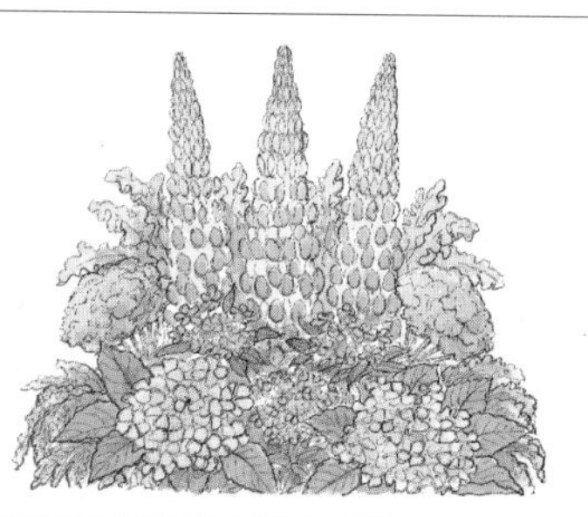

MAGNOLIA

Magnolia × soulangiana

Mostly deciduous, but with some evergreens, the hardy and half-hardy magnolia group of flowering shrubs and trees is renowned for spectacular flower displays. There are specimen magnolias for most sizes of gardens.

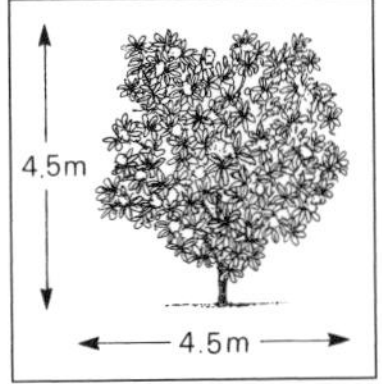

Suitable site and soil Magnolias like a deep, well-drained soil with added peat or leaf mould. Plant in a sunny spot; spring-flowering magnolias should be planted in a sheltered spot, perhaps against a wall.

Cultivation and care Plant out in spring and support with stakes until established. Top dress every spring with compost or peat.

AT A GLANCE

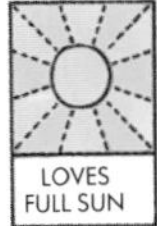

M. grandiflora

M. stellata

Propagation This can be slow and complex; most are bought as small plants. Propagation is by seed, layering or cuttings.

Recommended varieties The choice is largely dependent on what you have space for. One of the best medium-sized ones is deciduous *M.* × *soulangiana,* which has a height and spread of about 4.5m/15ft in time, and is usually smothered with large, rose-purple flushed white flowers in mid spring, before the leaves. There are named varieties with pink or purple flowers. Evergreen *M. grandiflora* is about the same size and has large bowl-shaped flowers from midsummer to early autumn. *M. stellata,* good for the smaller garden, is 3m/10ft high and wide at most and it has delicate white star-shaped flowers in spring. Although slow to grow, it will flower when young and does tolerate lime.

Pests and diseases Watch out for frost damage.

AGAINST THE WALL

M. grandiflora is very often trained against a south or west-facing wall where it gets plenty of sun and shelter from cold winds. It helps to train it if shoots low down on the plant are cut off in spring.

MATTHIOLA/*stock*

M. incana 'Giant Imperial'

This group of highly scented flowering plants is available as annuals, biennials and perennials. They are used as bedding plants in cottage-style gardens, and in containers. The flowers are suitable for cutting.

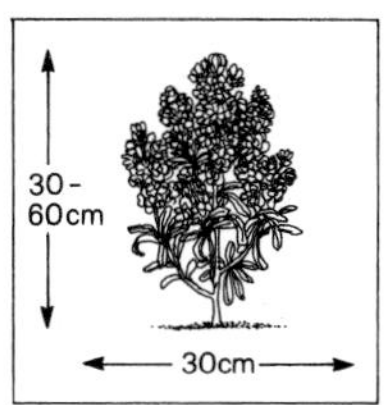

Suitable site and soil Plant in sun or partial shade with good drainage and in slightly alkaline soil.

Cultivation and care Stake tall plants in open sites. Cover biennials in winter and fertilize soil around them in spring.

Propagation Depending on variety treat as hardy annuals, half hardy in winter or as biennials.

AT A GLANCE

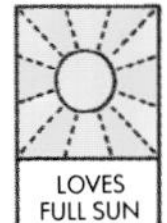

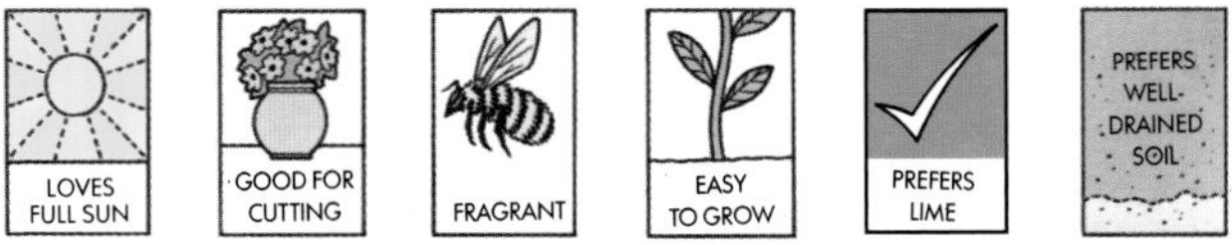

M. Brompton Stocks

M. bicornis

Recommended varieties Most garden hybrids derive from *M. incana*. Ten Week stock can be dwarf or tall with large flowers and comes in a wide range of colours, including pastel pinks, white, crimson, lavender and yellow. 'Giant Imperial' comes in burnished shades of copper, yellow and gold. 'Mammoth Column' grows to 75cm/2½ft and in summer has tall flowers, which are good for cutting, in mixed or single colours. Brompton stocks grow to 45cm/18in, have double and single flowers in pink, red, white, purple and creamy yellow. East Lothian stocks are bushy and grow to 30cm/1ft in a similar colour range. Trysomic and Selectable Double strains are fairly bushy and regularly produce double flowers. Trysomics are earliest to flower. For delicious evening perfume, grow the hardy annual *M. bicornis* (night-scented stock); its lilac-grey or purple flowers remain closed during the day but open at night.

Pests and diseases Prone to aphids, club root and mildew.

DOUBLE OR SINGLE?

Pick winning doubles from selectable variety seedlings. Those with pale leaves will produce double flowers. Those with dark leaves have single flowers. They are also early flowering.

MESEMBRYANTHEMUM/ *Livingstone daisy*

M. criniflorum

Shimmering colours and friendly daisy-like faces are the charms of these popular summer-flowering annuals. Use them as ground cover on a rockery, in summer bedding and across sunny and dry banks.

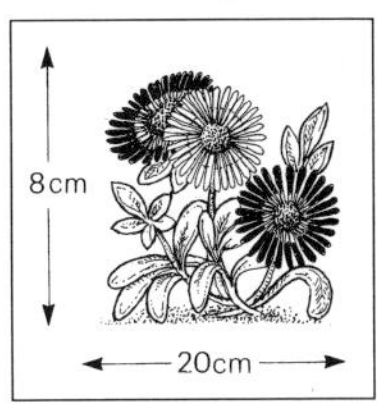

Suitable site and soil Plant them in full sun in well-drained soil. They do best in a light sandy soil.

Cultivation and care Plant out in early summer. Deadhead flowers regularly to prolong flowering.

Propagation Sow seed in spring into good seed compost in trays and provide gentle heat. You can sow direct into flower-

AT A GLANCE

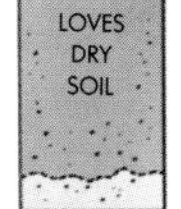

M. 'Magic Carpet Mixed'

M. occulatus 'Yellow Ice'

ing positions in late spring. When seedlings are growing well, thin out to leave 20cm/8in spacing between plants.

Recommended varieties *Mesembryanthemum criniflorum* is available as mixed-colour seed collections. 'Magic Carpet Mixed' offers a rainbow of pastel pinks, lilac and yellow to orange. Sometimes the flowers have a lighter shade or zoning near their centres. Botanists have changed this plant's name and it may be labelled differently. The new name is *Dorotheanthus bellidiformis.* For plain yellow flowers, choose another species *Mesembryanthemum occulatus* 'Yellow Ice' (also known as 'Lunette'). Its glowing flowers have a reddish central eye. It flowers early in summer and has a trailing habit that suits rockeries, edges or beds above walls.

Pests and diseases Generally trouble free, but slugs enjoy its leaves. It can succumb to foot rot, a fungal disease.

FAIR WEATHER FLOWERS

This sun-loving plant will not open if the sun is not shining. In wet weather, in the shade and on dull days it stays tightly shut. To get the best out of it plant it in full sun.

MYOSOTIS/*forget-me-not*

M. alpestris

A popular hardy biennial bedding plant, myosotis makes a delicate carpeting display. Use its tiny but profuse flowers to make a starry effect under spring bulbs or for early colour on a rockery.

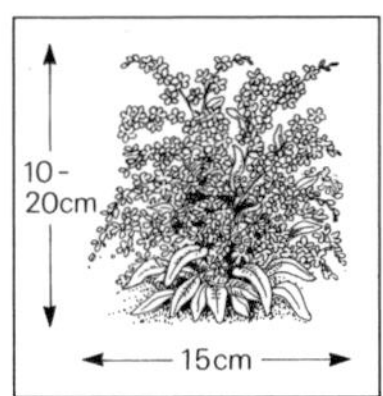

Suitable site and soil Plant in sun or partial shade in fertile well-drained garden soil, except for water forget-me-not which grows in moist soil as a marginal water plant.

Cultivation and care Water well in dry conditions and remove plants suffering from grey mould in wet, cold conditions.

Propagation Sow seeds in a seed bed outdoors in early

AT A GLANCE

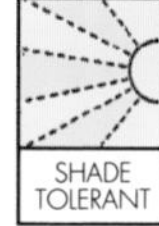

M. alpestris 'Carmine King'

M. *alpestris* 'Royal Blue'

summer and grow on in a nursery bed until ready for planting in flowering position in autumn. Self-seeds abundantly. Take basal cuttings from water forget-me-not, keep moist and plant out when rooted.

Recommended varieties Most garden hybrids are derived from the alpine myosotis, *M. alpestris.* 'Blue Ball' is good for edging and as a bedding plant. 'Carmine King' has rosy pink flowers and grows to 20cm/8in. Tall-growing to 30cm/12in, 'Royal Blue' is best as a dense planting in a mixed border. 'White Ball' is a compact plant that grows to 15cm/6in with a mass of white flowers. Water forget-me-not, *M. palustris* 'Blue Mermaid' grows in shallow water or a bog garden. It has a sprawling habit and produces small blue flowers in summer.

Pests and diseases Generally trouble free but in damp and cold conditions may suffer from grey mould.

CLASSIC COMPANIONS

For a perfect, fresh-looking spring bedding scheme, plan at least one bed with pink tulips blooming high above a delicately frothy carpet of blue forget-me-not.

NARCISSUS/*daffodil*

Narcissus 'Arctic Gold'

The yellow, trumpet-like flowers of narcissus mark the beginning of spring. Grown from bulbs planted in autumn, they are useful in mixed borders or in special cutting beds for use as cut flowers.

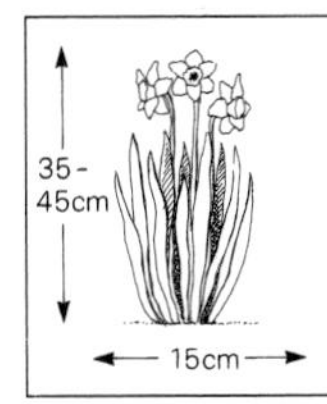

Suitable site and soil Plant bulbs in sun or shade in autumn into well-drained ordinary garden soil or pots for forcing.

Cultivation and care Plant bulbs deep in autumn. Deadhead flowers and leave foliage to die down naturally.

Propagation In autumn lift and divide large clumps, replanting directly. Young bulbs flowers in two years.

AT A GLANCE

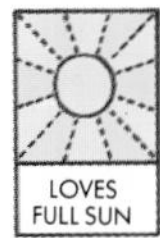

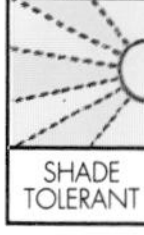

N. 'Golden Ducat'

N. 'Actaea'

Recommended varieties Daffodils come in various heights from miniatures or dwarfs which are just 8-15cm/4-6in tall to some of the tallest trumpet daffodils which can reach 50cm/20in. They may have double flowers, split-flower cups, large or small cups, or trumpet-shaped flowers. *N.* 'Arctic Gold' is a rich, yellow trumpet variety growing to 40cm/16in. Among the yellow and white narcissi, try the dwarf 'Little Beauty' or the taller, large-cupped 'Flower Record'. For a soft pink large cup, try 'Passionale'. Best doubles include 'Golden Ducat', 'Cheerfulness' and 'Tahiti'. Poeticus narcissi, such as 'Actaea', have small frilly central cups with red edges. Of the tazzeta narcissi, with up to 12 fragrant flowers per stem, try 'Soleil d'Or'. Jonquils also have several fragrant flowers on each stem; 'Suzy' has gold petals with an orange cup.

Pests and diseases Eelworm and slugs damage bulbs. Affected by several virus and narcissus fire.

THE NATURAL LOOK

Throw the bulbs gently onto the grass in the planting area so they have a random look. Make planting holes or lift a few turfs. Add fertilizer and cover with soil. Replace grass.

NEMESIA/*nemesia*

Nemesia strumosa 'Carnival'

These popular, bushy, half-hardy annual bedding plants make a colourful show in formal and mixed borders. In hot weather, blooming time is short and a later sowing will provide a succession of blooms.

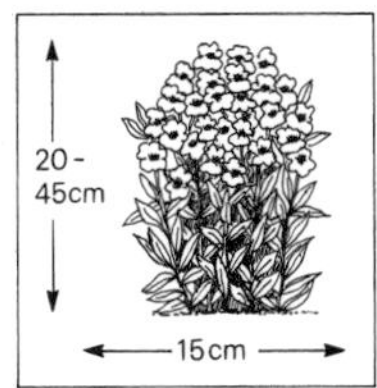

Suitable site and soil Plant in an open, sunny position or in light shade in well-drained and manured, slightly acid, soil.

Cultivation and care Plant out into flowering position in early summer and water well in dry conditions.

Propagation Sow seed into trays of compost under glass in early spring. When large enough to handle, prick seedlings off

AT A GLANCE

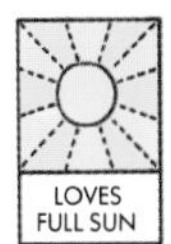

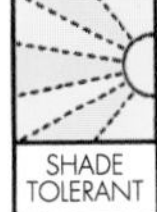

N. strumosa 'Blue Gem'

N. strumosa 'Fire King'

into boxes and harden them off before planting out in spring. In mild areas, sow direct into flowering site in mid-spring.

Recommended varieties *Nemesia strumosa* makes bushy growth and produces abundant flowers in a wide colour range. It varies in height from 20-45cm/8-18in. Flowers are trumpet-shaped and are available in white, yellow, orange, pink, red and various shades of blue. Seed is available in single colours, such as 'Blue Gem' and 'Fire King'. Mixed colour combinations are popular and include 'Carnival' with large flowers and 'Funfair'. Most unusual is 'Mello Red and White' with bi-colour flowers with top half red and lower half white. Also available is a plain white version 'Mello White'. For a collection of mixed bi-colours, grow 'Sparklers'.

Pests and diseases Generally trouble free but plants may die if attacked by fungal diseases such as foot and root rot.

SECOND FLUSH
When first flush of flowering is over cut back stems to produce a second flush of pretty flowers. At the same time, plant out second sowing of nemesia to provide an unbroken colour display.

NIGELLA/*love-in-a-mist*

Nigella damascena 'Miss Jekyll'

These popular annual flowers are best known for their pastel-coloured petals and feathery foliage spurs. Attractive in the mixed border and in flower arrangements, their dried seedheads can make winter displays.

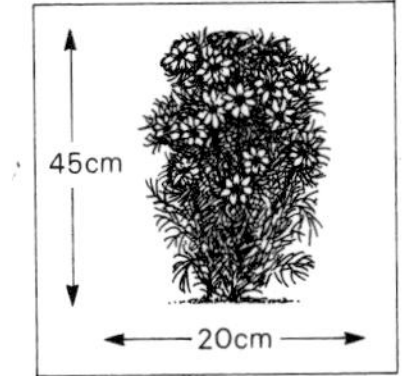

Suitable site and soil Plant in an open, sunny position in fertile, well-drained garden soil.

Cultivation and care Dead-head if seedheads are not required for drying, and to encourage continuous flowering and increase flower size.

Propagation Sow seed into flowering site in autumn or

AT A GLANCE

N. 'Persian Jewels'

N. hispanica

spring. Nigella self seeds abundantly if seedpods are left on the plant. Thin out seedlings to 23cm/9in in spring. In cold districts, seedlings may need winter cloche protection.

Recommended varieties *Nigella damascena* 'Miss Jekyll' has blue, semi-double flowers. Combine it with the white form 'Miss Jekyll Alba'. 'Persian Jewels', also with semi-double flowers, is a mixture of mauve, lavender, rose purple, white and blue flowers. 'Red Jewel' offers a single colour, deep rose. All suit mixed borders and offer an old-fashioned, cottage garden look. They grow up to 45cm/18in and need staking. For the front of the border, use 'Dwarf Moody Blue' which grows to 20cm/8in and makes an attractive path edge. *N. hispanica* grows to 60cm/24in with large, slightly scented blue flowers with red stamens.

Pests and diseases Generally trouble free.

CUT AND DRIED

Nigella seedheads make attractive material for dried arrangements. Cut from the plant just as the petals fall, strip off most of the feathery leaves along the stem and tie into bundles. Hang upside down to dry.

PAEONIA/*peony, paeony*

Paeonia officinalis 'Rubra Plena'

A group of mostly hardy herbaceous perennials and deciduous shrubs grown for their spring- and summer-flowering blooms and good-looking foliage. They are long-lived and once established should last for years.

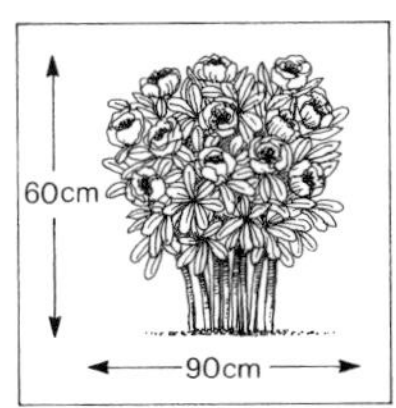

Suitable site and soil A well-drained but moist soil is best in a position in semi-shade, especially one that does not catch the sun first thing in the morning. Put in manure or compost before planting and plant shallow.

Cultivation and care Plant out in autumn or winter. No pruning is necessary but cut down herbaceous plants in early autumn. Put on a top dressing of compost or manure every

AT A GLANCE

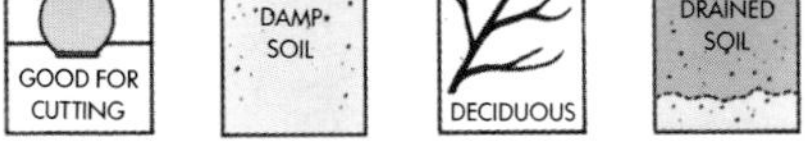

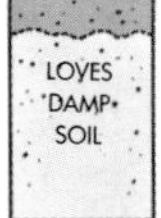

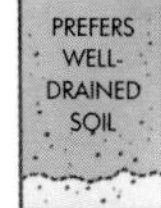

P. mlokosewitschii

P. suffruticosa

spring in poor soils. Remove faded flowers and in dry weather water frequently.

Propagation Grow from seed or by division in autumn. Shrubby species can be grown from hardwood cuttings.

Recommended varieties The traditional, herbaceous *P. officinalis* 'Rubra Plena' not only has beautiful deep red flowers but interesting foliage; it grows to 60cm/2ft. *P. mlokosewitschii* also grows to 60cm/2ft and has yellow flowers with darker centres in mid-spring; it also has interesting foliage. *P. lactiflora* 'Lady Alexandra Duff' has beautiful pink blooms. A good shrub is *P. suffruticosa* (tree peony), which grows to about 1.5m/5ft, or one of its varieties such as *P.s.* 'Mrs William Kelway' with white flowers in spring.

Pests and diseases Usually no problems with peonies.

PEONIES AND ROSES

Plant the scented *P. lactiflora* 'Lady Alexandra Duff', which flowers in late spring/ early summer, with shrub roses for a vivid and gorgeous display of contrasting plants.

PAPAVER/*poppy*

Papaver rhoeas

A fully hardy group of well-loved perennial, biennial and annual plants grown for their cup-shaped blooms. Most are easily grown from seed. There are poppies for the herbaceous border and for the rock garden.

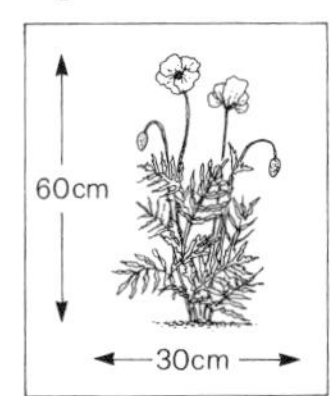

Suitable site and soil Most poppies are not too fussed about type of soil but they do best in a well-drained, rich, deep, sandy loam in a sunny position in a border. Rock garden species need a very gritty soil.

Cultivation and care Poppies are usually treated either as annuals or perennials. Generally they need little care but the perennial *P. orientale* needs staking while it grows.

AT A GLANCE

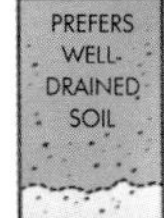

P. orientale

P. nudicaule

Propagation Most can simply be grown from seed sown in the flowering site but named varieties of the perennial *P. orientale* need to be propagated by root cuttings taken in winter if they are to remain true to their colour.

Recommended varieties *P. rhoeas* (the field poppy) is an annual and the 'Shirley Double Mixed', in mixed colours grown from seed in shades of red, pink, salmon and white, grows up to 60cm/2ft and spreads 30cm/1ft. *P. alpinum* (*P. burseri*, alpine poppy) is usually grown as an annual for rock gardens and has small flowers 2½cm/1in across. *P. orientale* (the oriental poppy) is a perennial growing to 75cm/2½ft. Forms of *P. nudicaule* (the Iceland poppy) are perennial but are almost always treated as annuals; they grow to about 60cm/2ft and make outstanding cut flowers.

Pests and diseases May suffer from downy mildew.

CUTTING POPPIES

Varieties of *P. nudicaule* (Iceland poppy) make good cut flowers when picked just as the buds open. Field poppies *(P. rhoeas)* are also suitable for cutting but the cut ends must be charred or they fade fast.

PARTHENOCISSUS/*Virginia creeper, Boston ivy*

P. tricuspidata 'Veitchii'

A small group of deciduous, woody-stemmed climbers grown mostly for their spectacular autumn foliage in hues of glowing red and bronze. There are species for sunny and sheltered positions.

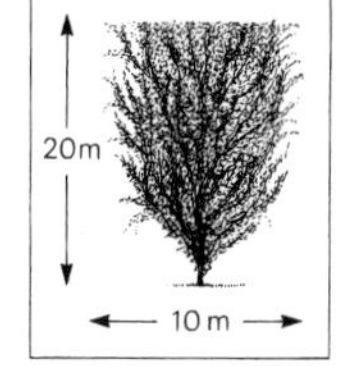

Suitable site and soil Grow in any well-drained soil in a semi-shaded or sunny site against a wall or up a tree with rough bark. They will also cover pergolas and fences. When planting, prepare the site by digging out a hole 60cm/2ft wide by 45cm/1½ft deep and fill with good soil mixed with compost or manure.

Cultivation and care Plant out during mild weather in

AT A GLANCE

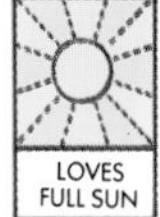

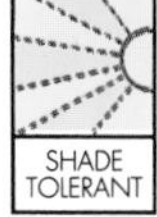

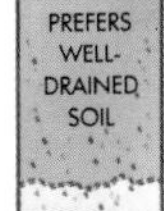

P. henryana

P. quinquefolia

winter. They do not need pruning but large plants can be reduced late in winter.

Propagation Increase by summer or autumn cuttings or by layers. They can, with some effort, be grown from seed.

Recommended varieties *P. tricuspidata* 'Veitchii' (*Ampelopsis veitchii*, Boston ivy) is a spectacular plant and covers large areas of wall, growing up to 20m/66ft. Its leaves are a glorious crimson in autumn and it also produces blue berries. *P. quinquefolia (Vitis quinquefolia),* Virginia creeper, is similar. *P. henryana* (*Vitis henryana*, Chinese Virginia creeper) does best in a shady spot but is less hardy than others. Its leaves are dark green until autumn but then turn light green, red and orange.

Pests and diseases Prone to aphids and scale insects.

GUTTERS AND TILES

In late winter the creeper can easily block guttering and even grow under slates or tiles on the roof, making leaks a possibility. Clear it from gutters and cut it back from roofs to avoid damage.

PASSIFLORA/*passion flower*

Passiflora caerulea

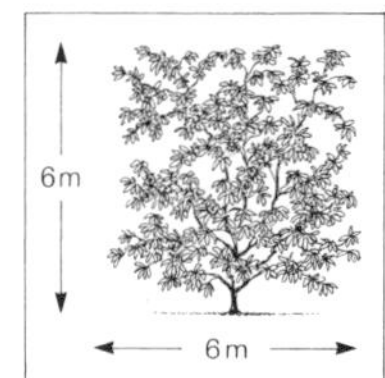

These evergreen woody-stemmed climbers are grown for their unusually shaped blooms and some produce edible fruits. Most are grown in the greenhouse but there are some hardy enough to survive outside.

Suitable site and soil Outdoors plant in well-drained ordinary soil in a sheltered position in a sunny spot where they can be trained against a wall. In a greenhouse, plant in a sunny position where they can be trained up a pillar or trellis in a tub or John Innes potting compost No. 3 or in well-drained, good soil in a greenhouse border.

Cultivation and care Plant outdoors in spring and in green-

AT A GLANCE

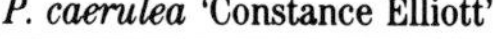

P. caerulea 'Constance Elliott'

P. edulis

houses in late winter. Water freely in spring and summer; water sparingly in autumn and winter. Keep above 7°C/45°F in greenhouse. Prune overgrown plants in late winter removing weak shoots; remove frost damage from outdoor plants.

Propagation Increase by semi-ripe cuttings with bottom heat in summer or from seed sown in greenhouse in spring.

Recommended varieties *P. caerulea,* with pink-flushed white flowers with blue banded crowns, climbs to 6m/20ft, is frost hardy and can be grown outdoors. A good variety is *P.c.* 'Constance Elliott' which has pure white flowers and is more hardy. Fruit producing *P. edulis* can grow in a greenhouse to 6m/20ft and has white and purple flowers in early summer.

Pests and diseases Not pest prone but may suffer the leaf deformation and discoloration of cucumber mosaic virus.

CONSERVATORY CLIMBER

In summer, *P. quadrangularis* has unusual green, white, pink and purple flowers. It makes a truly exotic display in a conservatory climbing up a pillar from a pot.

PELARGONIUM/*geranium*

Pelargonium 'Orange Ricard'

Of this group of plants, those most familiar to gardeners are the evergreen, tender, flowering plants grown as bedding in the summer and in pots. Some also have decorative or scented leaves.

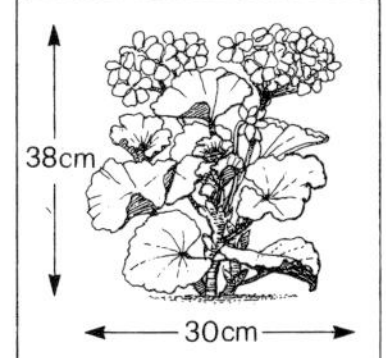

Suitable site and soil Most soils will do although they prefer a neutral to well-drained, slightly alkaline soil in a sunny position. Alternatively, plant in pots of about 13cm/5in in John Innes potting compost No. 2 or No. 3.

Cultivation and care Plant out from early summer and dead-head to prolong flowering. In pots, water freely in the growing period and sparingly in winter.

AT A GLANCE

P. 'Lavender Grand Slam'

P. tomentosum

Propagation Increase by softwood cuttings in spring and autumn or grow from seed.

Recommended varieties There are four main groups of pelargonium: zonal, regal, ivy-leaved and scented-leaved plants. Zonal plants are grown as summer bedding and in pots while regal are almost all grown indoors or in greenhouses. Just one of the immense range of zonal hybrids is *P.* 'Orange Ricard', with bright orange blooms. The typical zonal plant grows about 38cm/15in. The regal range has large flowers; one example is *P.* 'Lavender Grand Slam', growing to 45cm/18in. *P. tomentosum* (peppermint geranium) is an evergreen bushy species growing to about 45cm/1½ft, with leaves smelling of peppermint.

Pests and diseases Prone to a number of fungal and viral infections.

BASKET CASE

Ivy-leaved pelargoniums give shape and colour to hanging baskets. Trailing *P.* 'La France' has stems up to 90cm/3ft long and attractive, semi-double mauve flowers from early summer to late autumn.

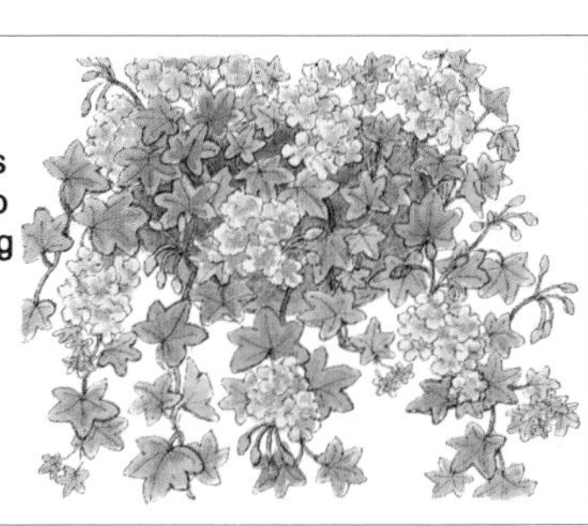

PETUNIA

Petunia 'Sugar Daddy'

Hybrids of this group of half-hardy perennials and annuals are almost always grown as annuals for their colourful and showy flowers. There are two main types: multiflora and grandiflora.

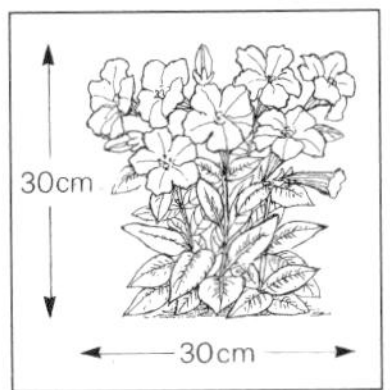

Suitable site and soil Plant in a sunny, sheltered position in fertile yet light, well-drained soil. If grown in pots, plant in John Innes No.1 in 13cm/5in pots. Alternatively put in tubs, hanging baskets and window-box displays.

Cultivation and care Plant out in late spring or early summer after they have been hardened off. Dead-head regularly to prolong flowering.

AT A GLANCE

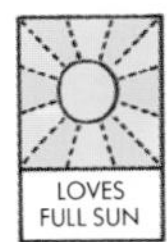

P. 'Red Picotee'

P. 'Dwarf Resisto Mixed'

Propagation Grow from seed sown under glass in early/mid spring at a temperature of 15°C/59°F.

Recommended varieties There is a large range of both types of petunia to choose from and all bear flowers profusely from early summer until stopped by a hard frost in autumn. Perhaps the best bedding plants are multiflora F1 hybrids sold in single and mixed colours; the 'Resisto' range is a good choice. Multiflora plants tend to be more weather resistant than the grandiflora type and have profuse blooms 5cm/2in across. Grandiflora F1 hybrids also give good displays in a bed or in a hanging basket or tub, producing larger blooms up to 13cm/5in across; the 'Daddy' series is popular.

Pests and diseases Watch out for aphids on growing plants and also for symptoms of viral diseases and cucumber mosaic virus.

CLEVER BOXING

There is almost nothing to beat a window box of petunias, in shades of pink, purple, red, white, blue or yellow; the flowers can be frilled, plain, striped and bordered. Plant 23cm/9in apart for best results.

PRIMULA/*primrose, polyanthus*

P. polyantha

This very large group of plants, suitable for a wide range of conditions, includes annuals, biennials and perennials which are fully hardy to frost tender. They are grown for their beautiful flowers.

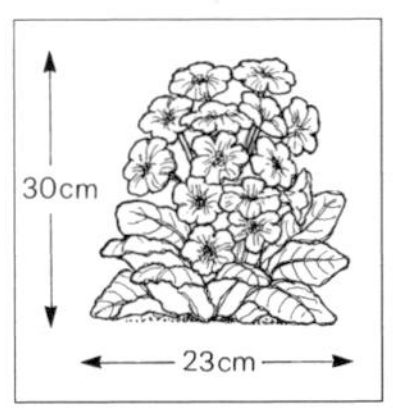

Suitable site and soil Essentially, there are three broad types: those that like ordinary soils in cool positions; waterside plants that like deep, fertile, moisture-laden soils; and alpine types which like sunny positions in open soil of sand, stone chippings and leaf mould.

Cultivation and care Generally, plant out between autumn and spring. Do not let alpine types dry out in summer.

AT A GLANCE

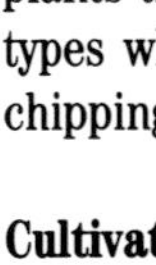

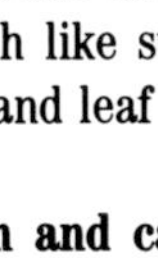

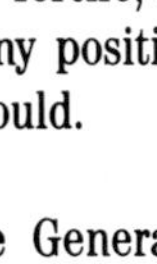

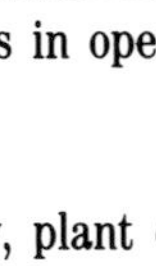

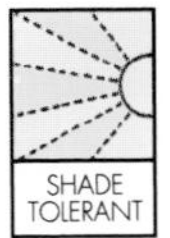

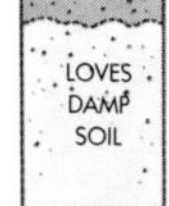

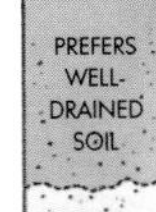

P. vulgaris

P. auricula

Propagation Grow from seed sown when ripe in gritty soil and peat. Well-established clumps can be lifted and divided in spring or when flowering has finished. Propagate *P. auricula* from offsets in spring or autumn.

Recommended varieties *P. polyantha* (polyanthus) is a favourite for normal conditions; it comes in a wide range of colours and grows up to 30cm/12in high. *P. vulgaris* (primrose) is another favourite for normal conditions. *P. auricula* (auricula) does well in alpine conditions and there is a large range of varieties available; they are fragrant and grow up to 23cm/9in. The moisture-loving *P. florindae* (giant Himalayan cowslip) grows up to 90cm/3ft high.

Pests and diseases Aphids and caterpillars can attack the leaves and weevils and cutworms attack the roots. The plants are prone to fungal, viral and bacterial diseases.

BEDDING PRIMROSES

Primroses make pretty bedding plants and look best beside a shady path or as the edging to a shady bed. Plant alongside scillas, tulips and other spring flowering plants.

PRUNUS/*cherry*

Prunus laurocerasus

This large group has many attractive ornamental trees and shrubs. The shrubs are grown for their flowers and fruits and the trees mainly for their flowers and foliage. Some are evergreen but most are deciduous.

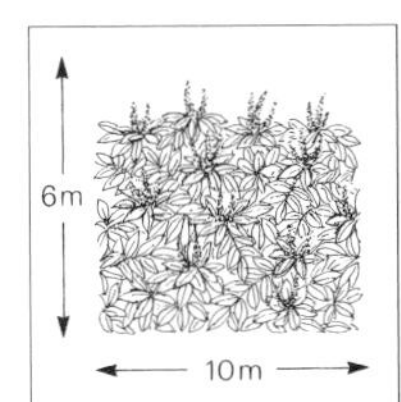

Suitable site and soil Generally, these plants do well in all except water-logged soil, but prefer a well-cultivated soil with a reasonable lime content. All like a sunny position and early-flowering varieties prefer a sheltered site.

Cultivation and care Deciduous species grown as hedges or shrubs may need a trim with secateurs after they have flowered in spring.

AT A GLANCE

P. persica 'Klara Mayer'

P. 'Accolade'

Propagation Deciduous species can be grown from seed in autumn while evergreens are increased by cuttings in summer.

Recommended varieties The evergreen shrub *P. laurocerasus* (cherry laurel) makes a fabulous hedge or screen. It grows to about 6m/20ft high by 10m/30ft wide and has leaves that are shiny above; it produces white flowers in the spring and the cherry-like fruits. The deciduous tree *P. persica* (peach), which grows to 4.6m/15ft high by 6m/20ft wide, comes in many varieties; one is *P.p.* 'Klara Mayer' which has vibrant pink flowers in spring. A good flowering cherry is the deciduous tree, *P.* 'Accolade', which has pale pink flowers in spring and leaves that turn bright red in the autumn.

Pests and diseases Birds may eat flower buds and aphids and caterpillars attack leaves. These plants are also prone to fungal diseases.

FLOWERS FROM A TREE

The bright and beautiful flowers of *Prunus* – often growing from bare woody stems – provide dramatic structural components in cut flower displays when artfully arranged.

PYRACANTHA/*firethorn*

Pyracantha coccinea 'Lalandei'

Plants from this small group of hardy evergreen spiny shrubs are grown for their flowers, produced in summer, their foliage and most of all for their clusters of spectacularly bright, autumn/winter berries.

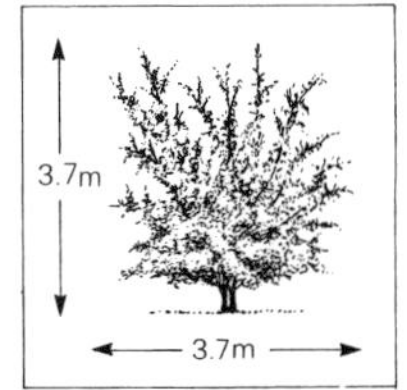

Suitable site and soil For a fine specimen, plant in an open site; alternatively plant against a wall, even a north-facing wall. They are not fussy about soil, as long as it is well-drained and fertile, and tolerate lime. They do as well in partial shade as they do in full sun.

Cultivation and care Prune side growths to maintain shape if planted against a wall. Plant out in autumn or winter.

AT A GLANCE

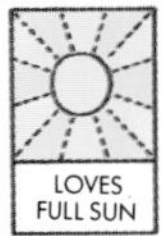

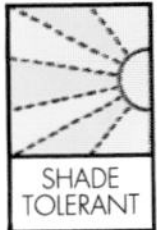

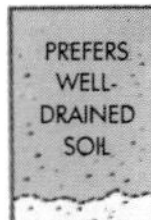

P. atalantioides

P. rogersiana flava

Propagation Increase by cuttings taken in summer and put in a propagating frame.

Recommended varieties One of the best is *P. coccinea* 'Lalandei' which has oval-shaped pointed leaves and produces clusters of small white flowers early in summer. These are followed by orange-red berries. It grows to 3.7m/12ft high and spreads 3.7m/12ft; 'Mohave' has a spreading growth and also produces orange-red berries. *P. atalantioides* is similar but grows to 4.6m/15ft and spreads 3.7m/12ft; it has white flowers and smaller but more numerous scarlet berries. *P.* 'Orange Charmer' is also similar but has orange berries. *P. rogersiana flava* is not quite so tall and has narrow, bright green leaves and white flowers that give way to yellow berries.

Pests and diseases Watch out for aphids and scale insects and also for fireblight and scab.

ATTACH TO THE WALL

When growing against a wall, firethorn does best if supported by wires or trellis. For optimum results, new, vigorous shoots need to be tied in during mid summer and early autumn.

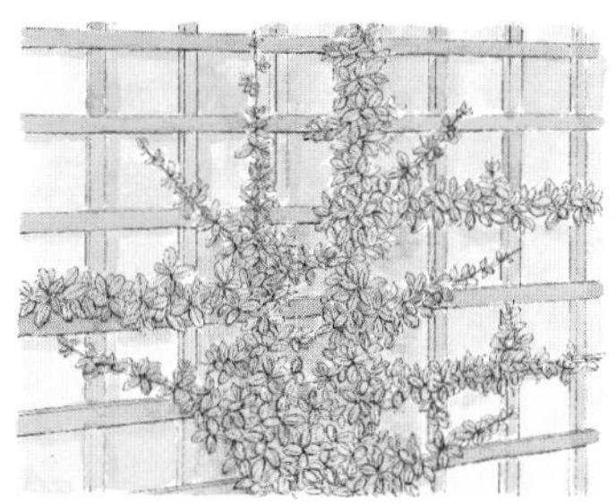

RANUNCULUS/*buttercup*

Ranunculus aconitifolius 'Flore Pleno'

Several of this large, mostly hardy group of plants, which contains herbaceous perennials, tuberous-rooted perennials and annuals, are useful for the border, the rock garden and for the water garden.

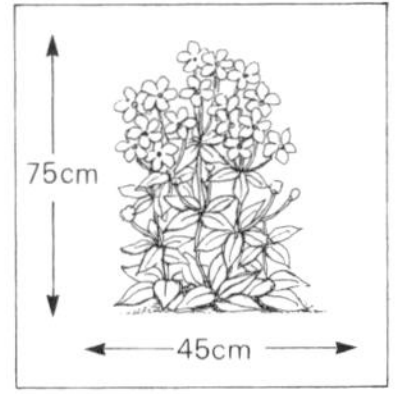

Suitable site and soil Plant all but aquatic varieties in well-drained soil in a sunny or partially shaded spot.

Cultivation and care Plant herbaceous and aquatic varieties in autumn or winter. Thin out aquatic species each spring.

Propagation Increase most by division in autumn or late winter. *R. asiaticus* tubers can be separated when lifted.

AT A GLANCE

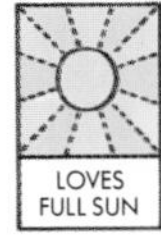

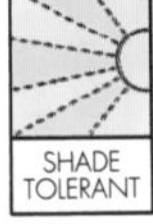

R. asiaticus

R. alpestris

Recommended varieties The herbaceous perennial *R. aconitifolius* 'Flore Pleno' (fair maids of France) grows up to 75cm/2½ft high and spreads to 45cm/18in. It has double white flowers, produced in late spring and early summer. Another good herbaceous perennial, based on the common buttercup, is *R. acris* 'Flore Pleno' which grows to 75cm/2½ft high and has double yellow flowers. The tuberous-rooted *R. asiaticus* (Persian buttercup) grows to about 40cm/15in and comes in a number of strains with, most commonly, double or semi-double red, yellow and white flowers 8cm/3in across produced in late spring/early summer. It spreads to about only 20cm/8in. A good rock garden variety is *R. alpestris* (alpine buttercup) with white flowers and glossy leaves. In the water garden, *R. lingua* has small yellow flowers in spring and grows to 90cm/3ft; it should be planted in 15cm/6in of water.

Pests and diseases Usually no problems.

LIFTING TUBERS

The tuberous R. asiaticus is not fully hardy. In cold areas it should be lifted in late summer, then dried and cleaned, before being stored in a cool, dry place for replanting in early spring.

RHODODENDRON

Rhododendron 'Dora Amateis'

This large group, which also contains azaleas, is made up of evergreen and deciduous, mostly shade-loving, shrubs and trees. They are grown for their gorgeous flowers and foliage and range from small shrubs to trees.

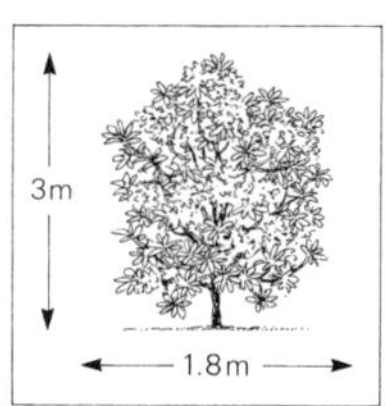

Suitable site and soil They need a well-drained yet moist, peaty loam with no lime in a semi-shaded, sheltered site.

Cultivation and care Spread fertilizer over the roots of the plant every year in spring and dead-head after flowering. Overgrown bushes can be cut back in late spring.

Propagation From cuttings, seeds, grafting and by layering.

AT A GLANCE

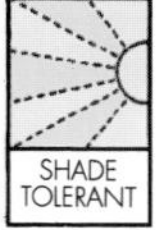

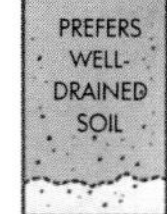

R. 'Purple Splendour'

R. luteum

Recommended varieties Hybrids are best for the garden as they are generally hardier and more tolerant of pollution. The evergreen compact *R.* 'Dora Amateis' has pink-tinged white flowers with green markings in spring. It grows to about 90cm/3ft high and wide. A popular showy variety is the evergreen 'Purple Splendour', with a height and spread to about 3m/10ft. It is fully hardy and has richly coloured blooms of an imperrial purple which appear in late spring and early summer. The deciduous azalea *R. luteum (Azalea pontica),* or one of its many hybrids, is a favourite and produces masses of yellow flowers in spring, with light green leaves turning scarlet in autumn. It is a vigorous shrub and grows to about 2.4m/8ft high by 1.5m/5ft across.

Pests and diseases Pests are weevils, caterpillars, whiteflies, and rhododendron bugs and leafhoppers. Diseases include powdery mildew, rust, honey fungus and leaf spot.

YELLOW, BLUE AND RED

R. luteum with yellow flowers in spring and scarlet leaves in autumn looks delightful when underplanted with blue flowers. Try willow gentian *(Gentiana asclepiadea)* in autumn.

ROSA/*rose*

Rosa 'Peace'

So popular is this large group of deciduous or semi-evergreen flowering shrubs and climbers that thousands of varieties are grown. Some might say that no garden is complete without at least one rose.

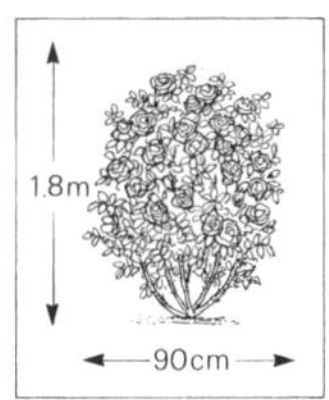

Suitable site and soil A rich medium loam in an open and sunny site is best. Prepare the site with well dug-in rotted manure or compost and dress the topsoil with peat.

Cultivation and care Plant out in late autumn. Keep watered during a dry spell in spring or summer. Feed about every three weeks during the growing period, apply a mulch in spring and prune according to type of rose.

AT A GLANCE

R. 'New Dawn'

R. moyesii 'Geranium'

Propagation Can be increased by seeds (species only), cuttings, budding or grafting.

Recommended varieties There are many types of rose and thousands of varieties to choose from. A classic rose is *R.* 'Peace' a vigorous hybrid tea rose that can grow to 1.8m/6ft and spread 90cm/3ft, with large scented, shapely yellow flowers tinged with pink. An excellent climbing rose is *R.* 'New Dawn' (see box). A fine modern rose is the floribunda *R.* 'Iceberg' which grows to about 75cm/2½ft high and spreads 60cm/2ft. It produces sprays of white double flowers through summer and autumn. A good species rose variety is *R. moyesii* 'Geranium' with scented, flat, blood-red flowers in summer. It grows to about 3m/10ft.

Pests and diseases Common problems are aphids, caterpillars, black spot, grey mould, powdery mildew and rust.

CONTRASTING CLIMBERS

Grow a climbing rose with another climber. A good mix is *R.* 'New Dawn', with *Clematis* × *jackmanii* 'Superba'. The pink of the rose and the purple of the clematis go well together.

RUDBECKIA/*coneflower*

Rudbeckia hirta 'Goldilocks'

This group of hardy annuals, biennials and herbaceous perennials are grown in the border for their vivid flowers with prominent central cones. They are also excellent for cutting and comparatively easy to grow.

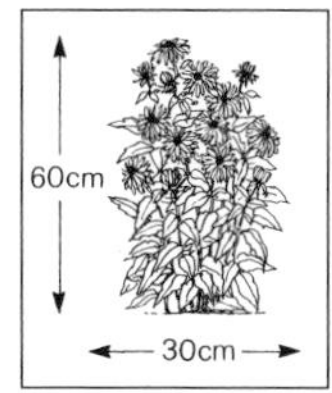

Suitable site and soil A sunny, open site and most types of well-drained soil suit these plants. Put smaller ones in the front of the border and taller ones towards the back.

Cultivation and care Perennials should be planted in autumn or early spring. Dead head frequently to encourage flowering. In windy positions, the taller plants will need support. Perennials should be cut down in late autumn.

AT A GLANCE

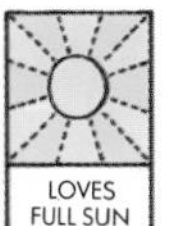

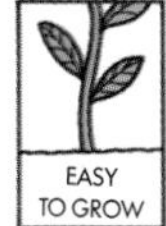

R.h. 'Rustic Dwarfs'

R. laciniata 'Golden Glow'

Propagation Grow annuals and perennials from seed and also divide perennials in spring or autumn.

Recommended varieties *R. hirta* 'Goldilocks', a perennial usually grown as an annual, is one of the best coneflowers, with its stunning double, golden-yellow flowers 8cm/3in across from midsummer to early autumn. The plant grows to 60cm/2ft and spreads 30cm/1ft. Another popular variety is *R. h.* 'Rustic Dwarfs' with flowers up to 15cm/6in across. *R. fulgida* 'Goldstrum' grows to 75cm/2½ft and its striking, yellow-gold flowers, produced in late summer, are up to 13cm/5in across with contrasting black cones. Taller is *R. laciniata* 'Golden Glow' which grows to 2.1m/7ft high and spreads 90cm/3ft, with double yellow flowers and greenish cones.

Pests and diseases Watch for signs of attack by slugs and snails; otherwise usually no problems.

GOLDEN VASES

Most types of rudbeckia make superb, long-lasting cut flowers. The long, strong stalks, bold, golden-yellow, large flowers and contrasting cones of *R. fulgida* 'Goldsturm' make it an outstanding cut flower.

SAXIFRAGA/*saxifrage*

Saxifraga × *urbium*

This group of hardy or half hardy plants contains annuals and mostly evergreen perennials. They are grown for their foliage and attractive flowers, and do well in rock gardens, raised beds, pots and troughs.

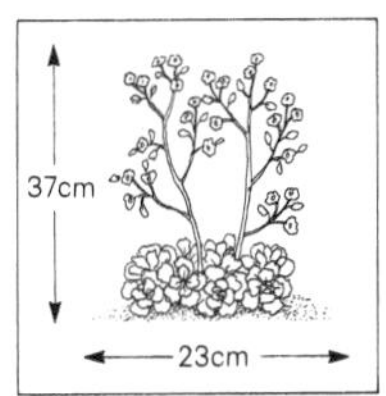

Suitable site and soil Generally, plants from the group should be grown in a sheltered site in semi-shade in soil containing grit; many prefer some lime in the soil. *S. stolonifera* as a houseplant or in a basket should preferably be potted in John Innes No. 1 or 2 potting compost.

Cultivation and care Most should be planted out in early autumn or late winter.

AT A GLANCE

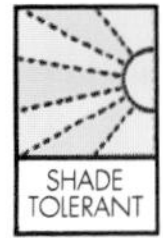

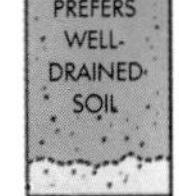

S. burseriana

S. stolonifera

Propagation Can be increased by growing free from seed in autumn or by offsets in winter or by division after flowering.

Recommended varieties The spreading *S.* × *urbium* (London pride) is a fully hardy perennial that grows to 30cm/12in. It flowers in early summer with masses of small pinky-white blooms on spindly stems; it is evergreen and its rosettes of toothed, oval-shaped leaves make good ground cover, especially in shady areas. Evergreen *S. burseriana*, one of the cushion saxifrages, grows slowly to 5cm/2in high by 10cm/4in across, with white flowers in early spring. It looks good in a trough garden. Evergreen *S. stolonifera* (mother of thousands) is used in sheltered rock gardens, in baskets and as a houseplant. It sends off runners bearing little plantlets which are easily used for propagation.

Pests and diseases Usually no problems.

THOUSANDS IN A BASKET

S. stolonifera looks superb in a hanging basket where its offshoots, called stolons, can trail down. Its leaves are an attractive deep green above and deep red or purple underneath.

Scilla

Scilla siberica 'Spring Beauty'

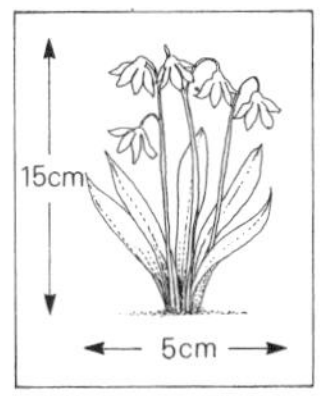

The plants of this group of hardy and half-hardy flowering bulbs are grown for their pretty blooms and glossy leaves. Some flower in spring and others in summer and autumn. They do well in grass and in rock gardens.

Suitable site and soil Plant 5cm/2in to 8cm/3in deep in any soil that is well-drained yet moist. The planting distance for the smaller plants such as *S. bifolia* and *S. siberica* is about 9cm/3½in and about 18cm/7in for larger plants, including *S. peruviana*. They thrive in sun or partial shade.

Cultivation and care After the bulbs have been planted in autumn they need very little care.

AT A GLANCE

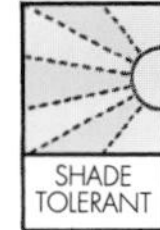

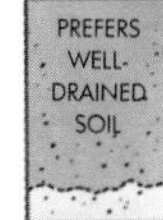

S. peruviana

S. scilloides

Propagation Can be grown from seed but more easily from offsets lifted in late summer and quickly replanted.

Recommended varieties *S. siberica* 'Spring Beauty' grows up to 15cm/6in and spreads 5cm/2in. It has striking, intense blue, bell-shaped flowers produced on stems in spring after the glossy leaves. *S. peruviana* grows to 30cm/12in and spreads to 20cm/8in; it produces dense heads of attractive, flattish, small blue flowers in early summer. *S. bifolia* flowers in early spring when each bulb puts forth a single stem with a number of star-shaped flowers which are usually blue but can be pink and white; it grows to 20cm/8in and spreads 5cm/2in. *S. scilloides* bulbs produce a spike of attractive small pink flowers in late summer and autumn; it grows to 30cm/12in and spreads 5cm/2in.

Pests and diseases Prone to fungal diseases, smut and rust.

BLUEBELL OR SCILLA?

The English bluebell was once named *Scilla nonscripta*. But it is now properly classified as *Hyacinthoides non-scripta*. It does, in fact, bear a great similarity to *Scilla siberica.*

SEDUM/*stonecrop, rose root, ice plant*

Sedum 'Autumn Joy'

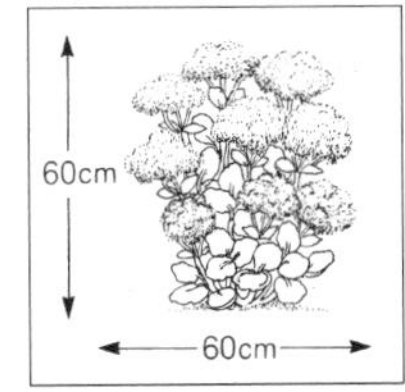

Plants from this huge group of succulent annuals and mostly evergreen perennials are grown for their flowers and their interesting leaf shapes. Many are suitable for rock gardens.

Suitable site and soil Plant in sun in well-drained soil.

Cultivation and care Plant out in autumn or winter. Most species are drought resistant.

Propagation Increase perennials by division in autumn or winter or by cuttings in spring. Annuals can be grown from seeds sown in early spring.

AT A GLANCE

S. spathulifolium 'Cape Blanco'

S. telephium 'Atropurpureum'

Recommended varieties S. 'Herbstfreude' (also known as 'Autumn Joy'), a hybrid of *S.spectabile* (ice plant) and *S. telephium,* is an herbaceous border perennial with fleshy leaves. It grows to 60cm/2ft high by 45cm/18in across and produces dense heads of deep pink flowers from late summer to late autumn. *S. spathulifolium* is a superb rock garden plant grown for its low (10cm/4in) spreading foliage of fleshy leaves. It produces yellow flower-heads in late spring; *S.s.*'Cape Blanco' has grey-white leaves. The fast-growing annual *S. caeruleum* produces star-shaped blue flowers in summer and grows to 15cm/6in. Its foliage turns red at the same time as flowering. *S. telephium maximum* 'Atropurpureum' has purple leaves which look dramatic in the border. It grows to 60cm/2ft and has large pink flower-heads in autumn.

Pests and diseases Watch out for attack by aphids, slugs and mealy bugs. Rot may occur where soil is too moist.

IMPERIAL PURPLE

Purple foliage can provide contrasting and complementary colour. *S. telephium maximum* 'Atropurpureum' looks especially good alongside the silvery-grey *Stachys byzantina (Stachys olympica)*.

Senecio

Senecio bicolor

This group of plants include annuals, greenhouse succulents, hardy perennials and shrubs, which are grown for their flowers and for their foliage. Many plants long known as senecio now belong to other groups.

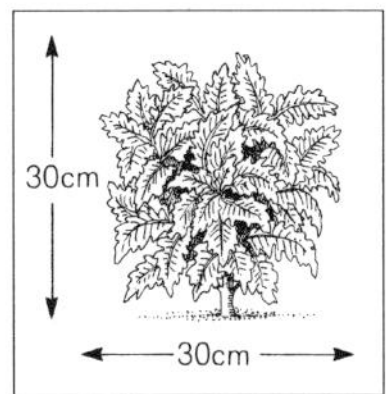

Suitable site and soil Annuals like sun and normal garden soil. Perennials like moist or boggy soil in partial shade. Succulents must be grown indoors. Shrubby types prefer well-drained soil and full sun.

Cultivation and care Plant perennials and shrubs in autumn or spring. Cut herbaceous types to ground level in late autumn.

AT A GLANCE

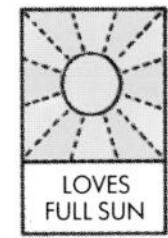

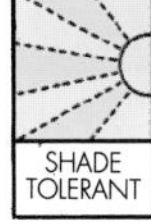

S. smithii

S. rowleyanus

Propagation Annuals are grown from seed sown in late winter. Perennials are increased by division in spring, shrubs from cuttings and succulents by cuttings taken in summer.

Recommended varieties *Senecio bicolor* (usually sold as *Cineraria maritima*) is a grey-leaved, half-hardy evergreen much used for bedding. It grows to about 30cm/12in with a similar width. Two popular hardy grey-leaved shrubs are *Senecio* 'Sunshine' and *S. greyi* (both now technically species of *Brachyglottis*). These grow to about 1.2m/4ft and have yellow daisy flowers in summer. Among the herbaceous types, *S. smithii* is worth growing, producing clusters of daisy-like flowers with yellow centres on 1.2m/4ft stems in summer. *S. rowleyanus* (string of beads) is a greenhouse succulent trailer with bead-like leaves.

Pests and diseases Watch out for aphids on all plants.

BOG LOVER

S.smithii is an excellent plant for moist, boggy conditions. Its striking leaves and clusters of yellow-centred, white flowers in early summer provide interest in an area where many plants do not do well.

SYRINGA/*lilac*

Syringa vulgaris

These hardy deciduous shrubs and small trees are grown mainly for their flowers which appear in late spring; many varieties are fragrant. They make good specimen shrubs, hedges and look well in borders.

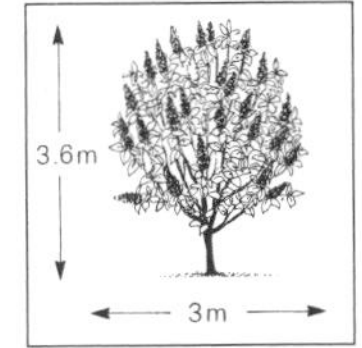

Suitable site and soil Sun or partial shade in a soil that is deep and fertile, preferably slightly alkaline, is best for members of this group.

Cultivation and care Plant out in autumn. Remove flowers as they fade and also get rid of untidy growth in autumn. In summer remove suckers, especially from grafted plants. Occasional removal of the old wood stimulates vigour.

AT A GLANCE

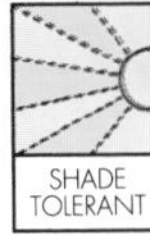

S. vulgaris 'Primrose'

S. meyeri 'Palibin'

Propagation Increase by heel cuttings in summer.

Recommended varieties There are many varieties of *S. vulgaris* (common lilac), a large shrub that grows to 3.6m/12ft high and spreads about 3m/10ft and produces fragrant, lilac-coloured flowers in clusters in late spring. Good varieties include *S.v.* 'Charles Joly' with single mauve flowers; *S.v.* 'Primrose' with creamy-coloured flowers; and *S.v.* 'Mrs Edward Harding' with red semi-double flowers. Bushy and dense, *S. meyeri* 'Palibin' grows to 1.5m/5ft high and wide with fragrant lilac flowers in late spring. *S.* × *josiflexa* 'Bellicent' is a disease-free variety that grows up to 4.5m/15ft high and spreads 3.6m/12ft. Its fragrant pink flowers in slim clusters are produced in late spring.

Pests and diseases Pests include caterpillars and lilac leaf miner. Diseases include lilac blight and silver leaf.

LILAC SCREEN

S. x. chinensis (Rouen lilac) makes an excellent screen. Plant about 1.8m/6ft apart and leave to get established. It grows to 3m/10ft, with attractive purplish flowers borne in late spring.

TAGETES/*marigold*

Tagetes erecta 'Climax'

This group of showy, half-hardy annuals includes some of the commonest and most popular border and bedding annuals. The flowers are produced from summer until autumn and also last well as cut flowers.

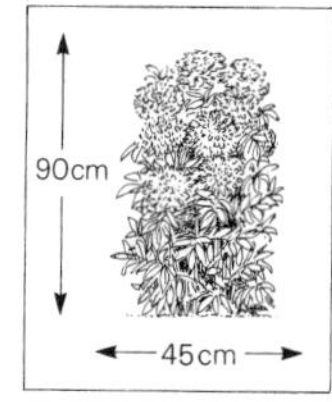

Suitable site and soil A rich, well-drained soil in a sunny position is best. Border edges are a good site for a row of marigolds.

Cultivation and care Plant out in late spring. Remove old flower heads to promote a longer flowering season.

Propagation Grow from seed sown in early or mid spring.

AT A GLANCE

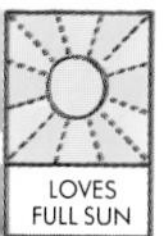

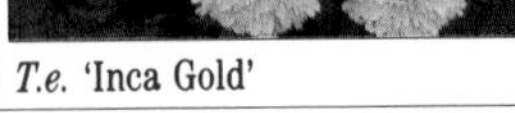
T.e. 'Inca Gold'

T. patula 'Disco Orange'

Recommended varieties Varieties of *T. erecta*, or the African marigold, are available in varying heights from 75cm/2½ft down to about 30cm/1½ft. Good varieties are the tall *T. e.* 'Climax', growing to 90cm/3ft and spreading 45cm/1½ft with large double yellow and orange flowers; and small African marigolds from the 'Inca' series which grow to 30cm/12in with gold, orange and yellow flowers. Varieties of *T. patula*, or the French marigold, are smaller and more compact. A good one is *T.p.* 'Disco Orange', with single flowers in a pretty, cheerful orange. It grows to 15cm/6in high and wide. Varieties of *T. tenuifolia pumila* (formerly *T. signata pumila*) make excellent edging plants growing to about 23cm/9in high and forming low mounds. They are available with lemon, yellow and orange-red flowers.

Pests and diseases Watch out for attack by slugs and snails; they may also suffer from fungal grey mould and root rot.

BUTTERFLY BALL

Varieties of *T. patula* (French marigold) attract butterflies. Plant them at the base of *Buddleia davidii* (butterfly bush) for a lovely swarm of butterflies and for a purple and orange flower contrast.

TROPAEOLUM/*nasturtium, flame creeper*

Tropaeolum speciosum

Most of the plants from this group are hardy climbers – some annual and some perennial – although in the garden many of the forms grown are dwarf or prostrate. They have attractive, brightly coloured flowers.

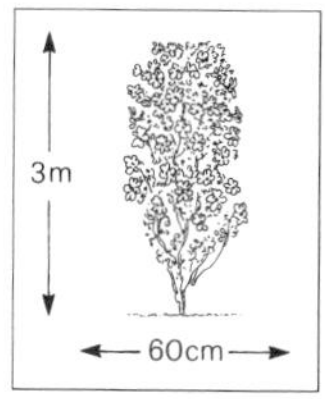

Suitable site and soil Most annual species prefer a well-drained, fairly poor soil in a sunny position. Of the perennials, *T. speciosum* prefers a slightly acid soil while most others are happy in any well-drained, rich soil in either full sun or partial shade.

Cultivation and care Plant out perennials in early spring. In cold areas, lift the tubers of tuberous species in autumn.

AT A GLANCE

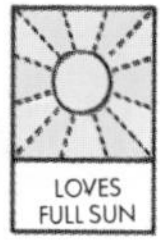

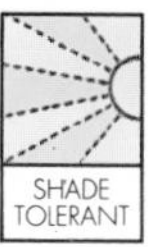

T. majus 'Whirlybird'

T. tuberosum 'Ken Aslet'

Propagation Sow seeds of annuals in the growing site in early spring. Divide perennials in late winter or, if tuberous species, lift and separate for the winter or when replanting tubers in early spring.

Recommended varieties *T. speciosum* (flame creeper, flame nasturtium, flame flower) is a really superb, fully hardy herbaceous perennial climber that does especially well in cool, moist climates. It has light green, six-lobed leaves and stunning flame-red flowers all summer long. It climbs to about 3m/10ft and spreads 60cm/2ft; its roots should be kept in shade. Good dwarf varieties of *T. majus* (nasturtium) include those of the 'Whirlybird' type in a range of colours. *T. tuberosum* 'Ken Aslet' is a perennial tuberous climber growing to 2.4m/8ft with red-orange flowers.

Pests and diseases Watch out for aphids and viruses.

THE HOLLY AND THE CLIMBER

Plant *T. speciosum's* straggly roots in rich, leafy soil at the foot of an evergreen shrub such as holly; it can then climb up the holly, with a dramatic colour contrast at flowering time.

TULIPA/*tulip*

Tulipa 'Apeldoorn'

What would the garden be like without tulips? These familiar, mostly hardy, spring-flowering bulbs come in a wide range of colours and, as well as being popular in the bed or border, make excellent cut flowers.

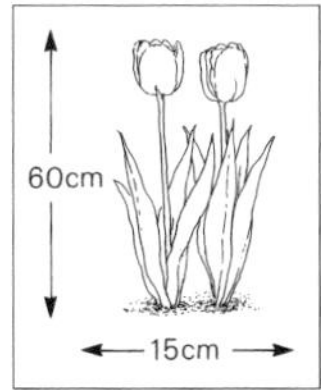

Suitable site and soil They do best in well-drained and fertile soil – preferably alkaline – in a sunny site.

Cultivation and care Plant out bulbs about 15cm/6in deep and 15cm/6in apart in mid to late autumn. Deadhead bulbs and remove petals from around the plant. Bulbs can be left in situ but it is best to lift them after the foliage dies back and store them in a cool dry place until replanting time.

AT A GLANCE

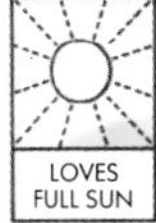

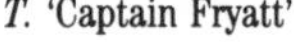
T. 'Captain Fryatt'

T. tarda

Propagation Increase from offsets obtained when bulbs are lifted. Species of tulip can be grown from seed.

Recommended varieties The range to choose from is huge. Tulips from the Darwin hybrid division give a good splash of colour in spring bedding. These grow about 60cm/2ft high and spread about 20cm/8in; of these *T.* 'Gudoshnik' is yellow and pink with red spots and *T.* 'Apeldoorn' is deep red. Of the lily-flowered types, *T.* 'Captain Fryatt' is the colour of red wine and grows to 45cm/18in. The Parrot types have unusual fringed flowers and *T.* 'Fantasy' is rose-pink with a green stripe. *T. tarda* is a good and attractive species that grows to only 15cm/6in high and has white flowers with a yellow centre; it looks good in a rock garden.

Pests and diseases Prone to attack by aphids and eelworms and a number of viral and fungal diseases.

TULIP TYPES

There are 14 or 15 divisions of tulip, of which three are distinct from the broad mass of tulips: parrot tulips, with fringed flowers; lily-flowered tulips with pointed petals; and double tulips.

VINCA/*periwinkle*

Vinca major

In the garden a few species of this small group of plants are grown for their ability to provide dense ground cover and for their delicate flowers. The ones cultivated are evergreen, invasive and hardy.

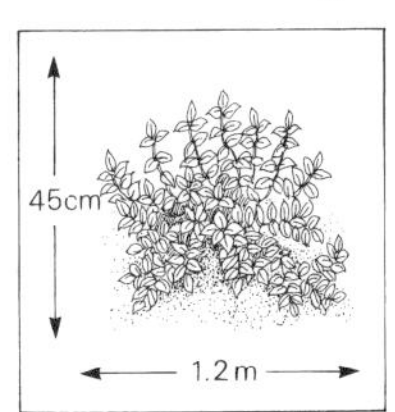

Suitable site and soil Any ordinary well-drained soil in a partially shaded spot will do.

Cultivation and care Plant out between early autumn and early spring. Generally easy to grow.

Propagation Can be divided from autumn to early spring and will also increase themselves by layering.

AT A GLANCE

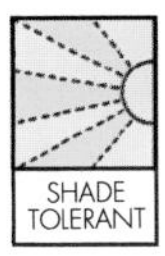

V. major 'Variegata'

V. difformis

Recommended varieties *V. major* (great periwinkle) is a robust, spreading, evergreen hardy sub-shrub with glossy oval dark-green leaves; it grows up to 45cm/18in with a spread of about 1.2m/4ft or more. It produces blue or blue-purple flowers about 2.5cm/1in across from mid spring to early summer. The variety *V. major* 'Variegata' has cream-edged leaves. Hardy *V. minor* (lesser periwinkle) is smaller at about 10cm/4in but with a similar spread to *V. major*. It too has glossy dark-green leaves, with its blue flowers appearing from early spring to mid summer. Good varieties are *V. minor* 'Aureovariegata' with yellow in the leaves and *V.m.* 'Burgundy' with wine-red flowers. *V. difformis,* another spreading sub-shrub, usually dies back in winter, but grows to 30cm/12in high by 90cm/3ft or more across.

Pests and diseases Usually pest free but *V. major* may suffer fungal attack.

PERIWINKLE ON THE LOOSE

V. major will grow almost anywhere, even in shade, and it is especially useful in a wild garden. To use as ground cover, space plants about 60cm/2ft apart for a really colourful spread.

Wisteria

Wisteria sinensis

These hardy, deciduous, woody-stemmed climbers are among the most attractive climbers. They are vigorous, with spectacular flowers in late spring and early summer. A large wisteria takes time to grow.

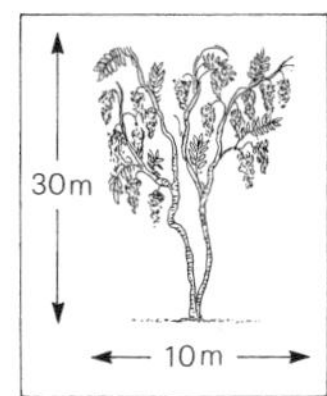

Suitable site and soil Most soils that are relatively fertile and that retain moisture will do. The plants must be planted in a sunny position and in cold areas do best against a south-facing wall where there is some shelter.

Cultivation and care Plant out in autumn or winter. These climbers need support and in late winter prune back hard to two or three buds on each shoot.

AT A GLANCE

W. floribunda 'Multijuga'

W. venusta

Propagation The most convenient method is to take heel cuttings in late summer. *W. sinensis* can be layered.

Recommended varieties *W. sinensis* is a truly superb climbing plant that can grow up to 30m/100ft high. It produces profuse hanging clusters of small, fragrant, mauve flowers in late spring and these look superb against the background of its bright green leaves. The variety *W.s.* 'Alba' has white flowers. Another excellent climber is the shorter *W. floribunda* which climbs to 9m/30ft. The variety *W.f* 'Multijuga' (this is usually sold as 'Macrobotrys') has 90cm/3ft long hanging clusters of purple-blue fragrant flowers. *W. venusta* is about the same size and has attractive clusters of fragrant white flowers with a yellow mark.

Pests and diseases Watch out for aphids and for fungal diseases that cause leaf spot.

SUPPORT FOR A CLIMBER

A large wisteria is a heavy plant and needs proper support both to get it established and to hold it in place. Make sure that fixings into masonry are sturdy and check them every year.

GLOSSARY OF GARDEN TERMS

alpine — A plant that grows naturally in the Alps; usually refers to plants suitable for rockeries, as these plants have a dwarf, compact habit.

annual — A plant that germinates from seed, grows, flowers, sets seeds and dies within a year.

aquatic — A plant adapted to living in water.

bed — A clearly defined plot within a garden.

bedding plant — Any plant that is used as part of a temporary garden display.

biennial — A plant that completes its life cycle in two years (and dies after flowering in the second season).

bog garden — A permanently wet, artificial garden, usually sited alongside a stream or water garden.

border — A cultivated area running alongside a path, wall or boundary fence.

bud — The growing point of a shoot.

burr — A seed head, flower case or fruit with bristles or spines.

bush — A low shrub whose branches all grow from ground level.

chipping — Nicking the outer coating of a seed, to speed up germination.

climber — A plant that ascends towards the light.

cloche — A moveable cover made from plastic or glass used for protecting early crops.

cold frame — A small, unheated permanent structure with a glass roof where seedlings can be hardened off.

compost — There are two types: the first is 'garden' compost, made from decomposed vegetable waste, grass clippings and other bio-degradable refuse; the second is a mixture of loam, peat and sand, used for potting.

conifer — Generally an evergreen tree or shrub that has needles and bears seeds in cones.

crown — The part of a herbaceous plant from which the roots grow down and the stem grows up.

cultivar — A cultivated variety of a plant; it differs from a naturally occuring variety.

dead-heading — Picking off dead flower heads to tidy plants and encourage further flowering.

deciduous — Refers to a tree or shrub which sheds its leaves in autumn or winter.

dibber — A hand tool for making holes in soil.

dormant	The inactive period, during winter, when a plant's growth temporarily ceases.
drill	An outdoor furrow in which seeds are sown.
dwarf	A miniature form of a plant.
evergreen	Refers to a tree or shrub which keeps its leaves throughout the year.
fertilizer	A substance that supplies nutrients to soil.
floret	An individual flower that forms part of a larger flower head.
genus	A group of closely related plant species.
germination	The sprouting of a seed.
grafting	Joining a shoot or cutting from one plant to the stem of another, to form a new plant.
ground cover	A carpet of low-growing, often spreading plants.
half-hardy	Plants that cannot withstand frost.
hardening off	Allowing tender and half-hardy plants that have been raised under glass to get used to outdoor conditions.
hardy	Plants that are able to withstand frosts; they can survive outdoors all year round in all but the most severe weather conditions.
herbaceous	Plants that produce soft, non-woody growth; they die down in winter, after seeding, and reappear in the spring.
humidity	The amount of water vapour in the atmosphere.
humus	Organic constituent of soil.
hybrid	A plant derived from crossing two varieties, usually of the same species or genus.
insecticide	Any substance, including chemical compounds, that will destroy garden pests.
invasive	Refers to plants which tend to become overgrown if not kept in check.
leaf-mould	A compost made from decayed leaves, that increases soil fertility.
loam	A rich soil consisting of clay, sand and decayed vegetable matter.
mulch	A layer of organic material or plastic spread on the soil's surface, around plants, to discourage weeds and preserve moisture in the soil.
nitrogen	The most essential element in plant nutrition.
organic	Produced without artificial chemicals.
oxygenator	Aquatic plant that releases oxygen through its leaves.
peat	Partially decomposed vegetable matter that retains moisture.

perennial	A plant that lives for more than two years.
pergola	A canopy or covered walk formed by plants trained over a series of arches.
perpetual	Flowering plants that produce blooms intermittently throughout the year.
pinching	Removing tips of unwanted growing shoots using finger and thumb.
pricking out	Re-planting seedlings into larger containers.
propagation	Increasing plants from seeds or cuttings or by grafting, budding, division or layering.
pruning	The controlled cutting back of branches to promote growth, encourage flowers and fruit, restrict size, or shape the plant.
screen	A wall, fence or hedge that encloses a garden or obscures an unattractive view.
seed leaf	First leaf or pair of leaves produced by a germinating seed.
seedling	A young plant, usually raised from seed, with a single, unbranched stem.
semi-evergreen	Refers to shrubs or trees which lose their leaves only in a very harsh winter.
shrub	A woody plant, smaller than a tree, with stems that grow from near ground level and no central trunk.
species	A class of plants that have common characteristics and that breed consistently true to type from seed.
specimen plant	Any plant that is grown in a place where it can be viewed from all angles.
succulent	A plant adapted to dry conditions, that has fleshy leaves and stems that store moisture.
tap root	A long, anchoring root that grows vertically downwards.
tender	Plants that are liable to damage from frost.
topiary	The art of training and clipping trees and shrubs into shapes.
tree	A plant with a central woody main stem or trunk.
variegated	Describes a leaf or petal marked with two or more distinct colours.
variety	A variant of a species arising naturally or through cultivation.
weed	Any plant that grows where it is not wanted, particularly when it competes with cultivated plants for light, moisture or food, or when it encourages pests and diseases.

INDEX

ACKNOWLEDGEMENTS

The publishers extend their thanks to the following agencies, companies and individuals who kindly provided illustrative material for this book. The alphabetical name of the supplier is followed by the page and position of the picture/s.

Abbreviations: b = bottom; c = centre; l = left; r = right; t = top.

Gillian Beckett: 26tr; Pat Brindley: 18tl, 19t, 20tl; Eric Crichton: 8tl, 22tr, 24tl, 162tl; Alan Duns: 11t, 12tr, 45t, 47t; John Glover: 26tl; Derek Gould: 8tr; Neil Holmes: 16tl, 24tr; Andrew Lawson: 22tl; Tania Midgley: 12tl, 84tr; Marshall Cavendish Picture Library: 13t, 14tl & tr, 20tr, 25t, 27t, 28tl & tr, 29t, 30tl, 33t, 37t, 40tr, 49t, 50tl, 52tr, 59t, 60tl, 61t, 62tr, 64tr, 65t, 66tr, 70tl, 71t, 72tl, 78tl, 80tr, 92tr, 93t, 100tl & tr, 109t, and all artworks; Photos Horticultural: 7t, 15t, 16tr, 17t, 21t, 30tr, 31t, 32tl, 34tl & tr, 36tr, 38tr, 42tr, 43t, 44tr, 46tl & tr, 51t, 53t, 55t, 56tl, 57t, 68tl & tr, 70tr, 72tr, 73t, 74tl & tr, 75t & front cover, 81t, 86tl & tr, 92tl, 95t, 96tl & tr, 97t, 98tl & tr, 99t, 101t, 102tl & tr, 106tl, 107t, 108tl & tr, 111t, 112tr, 113t, 116tl & tr, 118tl, 120tl & tr, 121t, 122tl, 123t, 126tr, 127t, 128tl & tr, 130tr, 133t, 137t, 138tr, 141t, 144tr, 146tl & tr, 147t, 148tl, 150tl & tr, 152tl & tr, 153t, 154tr, 156tr, 157t, 159t, 160tl, 162tr, 163t, 164tl & tr, 165t, 166tl, 167, 168tl & tr, 169t, 170tl, 171t, 172tl & tr, 173t, 174tr, 175t, 177t, 178tl, 181t, 182tl & tr, 186tr; Harry Smith: 9t, 10tl & tr, 18tr, 23t, 32tr, 35t, 36tl, 38tl, 39t, 41t, 42tl, 44tl, 48tr & tl, 50tr, 52tl, 54tl & tr, 56tr, 58tl & tr, 60tr, 62tl, 63t, 64tl, 66tl, 67t, 69t, 76tl & tr, 77t, 78tr, 79t, 80tl, 82tl & tr, 83t, 84tl, 85t, 87t, 88tl & tr, 89t, 90tl & tr, 91t, 94tl & tr, 103t, 104tl & tr, 105t, 106tr, 110tl & tr, 112tl, 114tl & tr, 115t, 117t, 118tr, 119t, 122tr, 124tl & tr, 125t, 126tl, 129t, 130tl, 131t, 132tl & tr, 134tl & tr, 135t, 136tl & tr, 138tl, 139t, 104tl & tr, 142tl & tr, 143t, 144tl, 145t, 148tr, 149t, 151t, 154tl, 155t, 156tl, 158tl & tr, 160tr, 161t, 166tr, 170tr, 174tl, 176tl & tr, 178tr, 179t, 180tl & tr, 183t, 184tl & tr, 185t, 186tl; Michael Warren: 40tl.

Index compiled by INDEXING SPECIALISTS, Hove.